The strongest men I k ... ts, acknowledge their less ... ir lives with the help of th ... .s heart the first time we met, and after reading *Who Am I?* I know why. Honest, gripping, and helpful are the words I would use to describe this book. His vulnerability will touch you, and his practicality will help you reach your destiny as a child of the King.

—Toby Slough
Mental Health Advocate and Founder, Goby Ministries

Who are you? How each of us answers that question shapes almost everything about our lives. In this intriguing and approachable book, Michael Carlton shares in an authentic and relatable way not only his personal pursuit of the answer to that question but also the truths that will guide each of us in answering that question in our own lives with intentionality and wisdom.

—Andy Lehmann
Executive Director, 415 Leaders

I am honored to call Pastor Michael a friend and leader in my life. He's the real deal on and off the stage. In *Who I Am?* Michael digs deep into his own life and struggles to give you a roadmap to find your true identity and purpose in Christ. If you've ever doubted yourself or battled with self-worth, this is a must-read. You'll walk away encouraged to live freely and fully in who your Heavenly Father created you to be!

—Kyle Hammond
Lead Pastor, Adventure Church, Columbus, Ohio

This is one of those "I know I need to read this, but I'm kinda scared, too!" kind of books! Michael shines light on the best question you can ever ask yourself: Who am I? If you are only going to read ONE book this year, make it *Who Am I?*

—Doug Garasic
Best-Selling Author and Pastor of Rust City Church

The journey to become all that God intended us to be is challenging. Add in significant issues from our family of origin, and you have an exponential challenge. This is Michael Carlton's story. In *Who Am I?* he reveals his journey of hurt, betrayal, and disappointment and how he came to the realization that God has written the days of his life, regardless of the choices his parents made. Michael's raw, transparent fashion leads into a practical framework for life. This is a book not just for those with hurt from their family of origin but for every Christ-follower who desires to find freedom and joy in spite of their circumstances.

—Jim Sheppard
CEO and Principal, Generis

When we are disconnected from who we really are, we will be disconnected from the world around us. Michael Carlton is one of the most authentic and real people I have ever had the honor to get to know and has such a passion to help others bloom into who they are created to be. When you know someone who knows who they are, it gives you permission to discover who you are. *Who Am I?* will take you on that journey!

—Bryan Briggs
Lead Pastor, Destination Church

Michael's story is memorable, powerful, and relatable. Having also been impacted as an adult by early family trauma, I was encouraged by his vulnerability and the practical ways he teaches how to navigate through trauma towards spiritual health. I highly recommend others read *Who Am I?* and find healing in their own lives.

—John Houston
CEO and Founder, John Houston Homes
Author, *Finding My Way Home*

Michael's journey is living proof that where you start doesn't have to determine where you end up. This book provides an incredible road map on how we can best navigate the liberating path of discovering our identity in light of Christ's deeper work in our lives. Through Michael's gripping account, you will find hope and confidence to live the greater purpose that God has in store for you. I can't recommend *Who Am I?* enough to anyone desiring to live to their full potential and overcome the many obstacles that can keep us stuck where we are.

—Chris Morante
Pastor, Evangel Church, Scotch Plains, New Jersey

MICHAEL S CARLTON

WHO AM I?

HOW I WAS RAISED WAS NOT
WHO I WAS CREATED TO BE

ARROWS & STONES

OTHER BOOKS BY THIS AUTHOR

*bloom.: A guide through the book of James to see
ourselves bloom into who we are created to be.*

Copyright © 2022 by Michael S. Carlton

Published by Arrows and Stones

All rights reserved. No portion of this book may be reproduced, stored in a retrieval system, or transmitted in any form or by any means—electronic, mechanical, photocopy, recording, scanning, or other—except for brief quotations in critical reviews or articles, without prior written permission of the author.

Unless otherwise noted, all Scripture references have been taken from the Holy Bible, New Living Translation, copyright © 1996, 2004, 2015 by Tyndale House Foundation. Used by permission of Tyndale House Publishers, Inc., Carol Stream, Illinois 60188. All rights reserved. | Scripture quotations marked **NIV** are taken from the Holy Bible, New International Version®, NIV®. Copyright © 1973, 1978, 1984, 2011 by Biblica, Inc.™ Used by permission of Zondervan. All rights reserved worldwide. www.zondervan.com. The "NIV" and "New International Version" are trademarks registered in the United States Patent and Trademark Office by Biblica, Inc.™ | Scripture quotations marked **NKJV** are taken from the New King James Version®. Copyright © 1982 by Thomas Nelson. Used by permission. All rights reserved. | Scripture quotations marked **MSG** are taken from THE MESSAGE, copyright © 1993, 1994, 1995, 1996, 2000, 2001, 2002 by Eugene H. Peterson. Used by permission of NavPress. All rights reserved. Represented by Tyndale House Publishers, Inc. | Scripture quotations marked **ESV** are from The ESV® Bible (The Holy Bible, English Standard Version®), copyright © 2001 by Crossway, a publishing ministry of Good News Publishers. Used by permission. All rights reserved. | Scripture quotations marked **TPT** are from The Passion Translation®. Copyright © 2017, 2018 by Passion & Fire Ministries, Inc. Used by permission. All rights reserved. ThePassionTranslation.com. | Scripture quotations marked **CSB** have been taken from the Christian Standard Bible®, Copyright © 2017 by Holman Bible Publishers. Used by permission. Christian Standard Bible® and CSB® are federally registered trademarks of Holman Bible Publishers.

For foreign and subsidiary rights, contact the author.

Cover design by: Sara Young

Cover Photo by: John Michael Judah

ISBN: 978-1-957369-29-7   1 2 3 4 5 6 7 8 9 10

Printed in the United States of America

Dedication

This book is dedicated to my beautiful wife, Amanda. You have shown me what a loving family looks like, and you have brought so much healing to my life. Thank you for helping me be a better father, husband, leader, and pastor. Penguin, you are my best friend, and I love you with my everything! And to my beautiful children—Kingston, Major, and Londyn—you three truly are a gift from God, and you have brought so much joy into your mother's and my life. Thank you for making our family complete. Your daddy loves you with his whole heart!

FOREWORD

I'm so impressed with Mike Carlton. He's one of the most gifted and humble pastors I know. God has taken him through a lot of heartache and stress, and he has learned very valuable lessons—many of which he shares in this book. For instance, all of us have emotional and relational wounds, but until we're honest about them, exposing them to the light of God's love and truth, they'll be a wet blanket on our growth, our leadership, and our relationships. I know because I've been there.

Like it was for a lot of people, my high school years were full of glorious highs and unspeakable lows. On the positive end of the spectrum, I met my wife Jenni when we were in *Fiddler on the Roof*. Every day, I sang to her, "Matchmaker, matchmaker, make me a match." And the real Matchmaker eventually did just that, but it certainly wasn't because I impressed her with any athletic talent. That's on the other end of the spectrum. During my freshman year, I tried out for the basketball team at my new school. Before I tell this story, let me give you a little background: My parents had taken me out of public school and enrolled me in a private Christian school because they were afraid I was heading in the wrong direction spiritually. They had only one data point, but it was enough for them: At the end of my eighth grade year, one of my friends invited me to her birthday dance party in the garage at her home. I really wanted to go, but my dad growled, "Son, you know how we feel about dancing." (It's hard to express the extent of my parents' animosity against dancing. I have the sneaking suspicion their primary reason to be against premarital sex was because it might lead to dancing!) Dad wanted me to hear from God, so he told me, "Go to your room and ask God what He thinks about you going to the dance."

A few minutes later, I walked back into the room and told Dad, "I think God is good with it."

He wasn't happy. He shook his head and said, "Well, that tells me where you are, son. You aren't spiritually mature enough to hear the voice of God."

I begged and pleaded, and eventually, my dad let me go, but only for an hour. When he picked me up, the music was blaring from the garage. As soon as I closed the door to the car, he asked, "So, how do you feel about it now? It wasn't what you expected, was it?"

I replied, "Not at all. It was better than I could have ever imagined!"

That was the moment when my dad decided I needed to go to a Christian high school, and it was during that first year that I tried out for the basketball team. I'd never played competitive basketball in school, but I thought, *How hard could it be?* I'd played with the other Royal Rangers (like Christian Boy Scouts) at our church on Wednesday nights. I was the best player on the court—I was the Lebron James of the Pioneers!

At the first tryout in my new school, I put on my gym shorts and shoes, and joined the other guys gathered around the coach. The first thing out of his mouth was, "Let's do the weave drill." The weave drill? I'd never heard of it. We had never done a weave drill in Royal Rangers. I saw some boys running and passing the ball, but it didn't make any sense to me. I didn't want to be embarrassed in front of all the other guys, so I acted like I had to go to the bathroom and left the court . . . and I left the gym. I called my Mom to pick me up. While I waited for her, the enemy used the fertile soil of my shame to plant a lie: He didn't say, "You're not good enough at basketball to make the team ... no ... that was true. He said, "You're not good enough ... you're a loser ... don't ever try to do anything great because you'll just fail. You'll look stupid, and everyone will know you're a loser!" I believed this soul-crushing lie from the enemy for more than a decade.

Internalized lies from the enemy seldom exist in isolation; they're usually coupled with an inner vow. The lie was, "I'll never be good enough. I'm a loser," and the vow was a commitment to self-protection: "I'll never again put myself in a position to look stupid like that." The lie and the vow were the ingredients for the enemy to erect a stronghold in my mind and heart. It was more real to me than any truth I heard or read. Let me explain how these pieces fit together:

→ A core lie is a false belief implanted by the enemy—usually through experiences of fear, anger, hurt, or shame—which becomes the lens through which we see every person and every situation.
→ The vow is a coping strategy to minimize the risk of being devastated again, and it dictates our responses to every circumstance: fighting any perceived threat, running from any risk of failure, or pleasing people to win their approval but losing ourselves in the bargain. (And if we're really creative, all of these!)
→ The stronghold is the tightly constructed false perceptions and defense strategies that become a form of bondage, limiting (or crushing) hopes for love, joy, and freedom.

It took a long time, but eventually, God used some loving, wise mentors and authors to help me conquer my stronghold. One day as I prayed that God would help me overcome my insecurity and fear, He took me back to that day at the basketball tryouts and taught me three essential Rs to breaking the strongholds in my life:

→ Recognize the stronghold for what it is.
→ Reject the lie and the vow.
→ Receive God's gracious, affirming, forgiving truth.

The battle for our minds and hearts isn't a quick fight . . . it's siege warfare, which takes time, intention, and perseverance. Paul explained:

> *For though we walk in the flesh, we do not war according to the flesh.*
> *For the weapons of our warfare are not carnal but mighty in God*
> *for pulling down strongholds, casting down arguments and every*
> *high thing that exalts itself against the knowledge of God, bringing*
> *every thought into captivity to the obedience of Christ.*
> —2 Corinthians 10:3-5 (NKJV)

Strongholds appear indestructible, but they're not. They appear permanent, but they can be demolished by sustained, tenacious, Spirit-drenched, Word-empowered, mentor-inspired battle. We fight to identify the foothold the enemy has gained when we believed the core lie and used the vow to protect ourselves from further hurt. We win by examining the thoughts in our minds, rejecting what's not from God, and feasting on our identity as God's treasured sons and daughters.

As you read Mike's book, you'll be inspired by his honesty and challenged by his courage. Don't miss what God wants to say to you in these pages. Who knows? God may use this book to help you break the strongholds that have been holding you back from becoming all He created you to be.

—Scott Wilson
Global Pastor, Oaks Church
Founder and CEO of 415Leaders & RSGLeaders
Author, *Identity: The Search*

CONTENTS

CHAPTER 1

BEGINNINGS ARE IMPORTANT. BUT HOW YOU FINISH IS *MORE* IMPORTANT.

In one of his countless leadership books, John Maxwell states, "If you have good values on the inside, the less you need validation on the outside." Now, while I love this pithy statement, it does leave you with a gnawing question or two. First, how do you get good values on the inside? Secondly, how did we get those bad values in there in the first place? Well, let's answer these questions by first starting with the latter.

Bad values, in my opinion, are not something you are born with but something you acquire over time. Unfortunately, we acquire many in our formative years that we use as a foundation of who we claim our identity to be. With these unhealthy tools, we think we can protect and provide for ourselves throughout our lifetime. Much of this providing and protecting is less about the physical and much more about our emotional and mental selves. How do we keep ourselves from getting hurt, and how do we make ourselves feel good? These become self-conscious motivators that drive our decisions and regulate our emotions.

You may think this is a simplistic explanation to a complex psychological understanding, and it is—to a point. Still, it is also incredibly accurate when you think about why you dream, behave, and interact with others the way you do. As humans, the last thing we want is for some form of harm to happen to us, and the thing we want most is to have our deepest needs met.

> As humans, the last thing we want
> is for some form of harm to happen
> to us, and the thing we want most is
> to have our deepest needs met.

The negative values come into play when we start to view these two desires through the wrong lens based on what we have experienced and what has been modeled for us by those of influence in our lives. When someone of influence hurts us physically and emotionally, we do one of two things. For the sake of not being hurt again as we go through this life, we keep good people at arm's length. In return, we miss the intimacy of genuinely authentic and vulnerable relationships.

At the other extreme, we confuse abuse with love and go from one abusive relationship to another because we tragically believe that abuse equals attention which equals love. Building off of that understanding, from our formative years, we see those we look up to chase after unhealthy things in the name of feeling good. Because of this, we develop a wrong understanding of what true pleasure is and spend our adult years chasing after the wind, living in a constant state of disappointment as it is uncatchable.

The greatest tragedy of all is that most of us have no concept that we are doing this. These unhealthy motivators have been so ingrained into our identity that we believe it is normal. Not only do we believe our reactions are normal, but we are now trained in a world that is putting out a plethora of highlight reels on social media that make us believe the answer to feeling better is to change our situation. A new job, spouse, vacation, car, house, etc., etc., will actually make all that deep pain go away. So we look outward for our answers instead of inward. In his legendary book, *Run with the Horses*, Eugene Peterson sums it up perfectly when he says:

The outside is a lot easier to reform than the inside. . . . We live in a culture where image is everything and substance nothing. We live in a culture where a new beginning is far more attractive than a long follow-through. Images are important. Beginnings are important. But an image without substance is a lie. A beginning without continuation is a lie.[1]

It is so easy to try to suck it up and move on. Just forget it. Start over. Try something new. In doing so, we think we are blank slates embracing new experiences, but we are actually carrying a ton of hidden baggage with us. Until we become truly honest with ourselves and work through some of the hurts we have accumulated through the years, especially pain from our childhood, every new beginning we set out on will end in the same tragic disappointments we have been escaping.

This is why I am writing this book as I navigate through some of the memories from my childhood and discover the defense mechanisms that I have accumulated over the years because of a survival instinct. I hope to help you understand that, first, you are not alone. It is easy to find ourselves locked in an internal cell of isolation, thinking that no one understands us. We can feel that we have always had to fight our battles alone and that we always will. It is true: the circumstances you have faced are unique and, unfortunately, yours. What is not true is that hardships are uniquely yours, and the weight you carry can only be borne alone.

Secondly, as you give your mind permission to feel and recognize what you have gone through in the past, your brain may start releasing memories that you have subconsciously suppressed for many years. Remember, our psyche tries to protect us from pain. Still, in doing so, we sometimes develop unhealthy responses and reactions in life that affect how we interact with others, how we handle responsibilities, or how we navigate stressful situations. We tend to do these things from

---

1 Eugene H. Peterson and Eric E. Peterson, *Run with the Horses: The Quest for Life at Its Best* (Downers Grove, IL: IVP Books, 2019).

a subconscious state because these memories have been suppressed, but our subconscious still reacts.

I do not know if you have ever had those thoughts of desperation where you cannot understand why you keep reacting or behaving a certain way when you know it is wrong, but you feel like you cannot stop doing it. We must bring to light why we get triggered and the cause of our deep pain. The devil understands this, and he loves for you to keep your secrets locked up on the inside; the manipulator that he is understands true healing comes from bringing to light those pain points. That is why James writes so powerfully, "Confess your sins to each other and pray for each other so that you may be *healed*" (James 5:16, emphasis added).

Now, I know what you may be thinking: *I did not sin because I did nothing wrong. I am the victim!* Listen to me very clearly; sin is not just a moral issue but any decision that keeps us from walking in the design of God. Some of us decide to carry a weight that we have no business carrying, hold mindsets that are opposite of the mind of God, and speak words over ourselves or others that are filled with death, not life. We have to bring them to light in the context of a healthy community to drive us out of isolation, move us away from the lies, and lead us toward our God and His design for our lives.

Some of us decide to carry a weight that we have no business carrying, hold mindsets that are opposite of the mind of God, and speak words over ourselves or others that are filled with death, not life.

Lastly, I hope you see the importance of a healthy therapist that can help you navigate your story, pinpoint those sensitive areas in your life, and help you learn to react in health. Do not believe the devil who is the father of lies. That manipulator will tell you just to suck it up and get over yourself and that therapy is for the weak, that you are stronger than that. The enemy will tell you that it is nobody's business but yours and that you do not need to confess to anyone because he does not want you to walk in the healing that James talks about. Jesus said it best when describing the devil's motivation, "The thief's [devil's] purpose is to steal and kill and destroy. My purpose is to give them a rich and satisfying life" (John 10:10). The devil wants to steal your joy, kill your purpose, and destroy your relationships, but God's way is to make sure your life and your relationships are rich and satisfying. We have to navigate our lives biblically, not emotionally.

So as I navigate through some of my childhood memories and the defense mechanisms I have accumulated, my goal is not to paint my family in a negative light. My parents were just responding to life from the accumulation of what they experienced growing up. They were reacting, though many times in unhealthy ways, through their subconscious survival instinct. However, I want to clearly paint the picture of why we see the world the way we do through real-life experiences and how a series of incidents that may even be decades old can still play a vital role in our present-day lives. Remember what the goal is. The goal is not to be a victim, blame others, get vengeance, or keep living in the past. The goal is to identify pain points, connect how they are playing out in your present life, and determine how you can healthily move beyond them.

I hope you know that what happened to you as a child may not be your fault, and you may have been grossly mistreated by those that were supposed to protect and care for you. However, what you do as an adult is your responsibility. It is your responsibility to change negative mindsets and behaviors, so you do not let the hurts that you have accumulated come crashing down on those that you love. No, you cannot hop in a time machine and stop those tragedies from happening. Still, you can face them head-on. Then, through Godly voices and, most importantly, the move of a loving God in your life, you can not only find healing, but you can now be a testimony of change that can bring healing into the lives of many others.

I always say the greatest gift that God gave us was not Jesus; the greatest gift God actually gave us was the ability to *choose* Jesus. Free will is the greatest gift God gave us because love cannot be forced; it must be chosen. God has already chosen you, but you must choose Him. You must choose His forgiveness, His Lordship, His healing, and His plan for your life.

Free will is the greatest gift God gave us because love cannot be forced; it must be chosen.

There are a series of choices you will have to make to discover the freedom you were created to have. God does not expect you to be perfect or to have a perfect life, but He also does not expect you to settle for a life you were never intended to call your own. God is not asking for perfection, just progression. Progress every day is taking a step at a time to get closer to the healthy person of purpose lying dormant inside of you. Yes, you may have some challenges to overcome based on what you experienced growing up. However, remember this: that may be how you were raised, but it is NOT who you were created to be!

CHAPTER 2

NOT ME; I AM GOOD!

This could possibly be the most cliché statement I will make, but here goes nothing: I remember it like it was yesterday. It is the day and the moment that would take me on a journey that I did not know I even needed. This moment occurred while my wife and I were sitting in a conference room at a boutique hotel in downtown Dallas with four other pastor couples in August of 2019. Amanda and I were at a retreat led by Pastor Scott and Jenni Wilson, who were at the time becoming two of my most significant influences. His director, Andy Lehmann, and his wife, Lindsey, were there with us as well. Honestly, I thought I was there to help start a network for church planters that would help pastors not only launch their churches but also have a support system around them to see their churches grow into healthy ministries. I went into this retreat thinking only about what I could give, not knowing I would leave receiving more than I could ever have expected to get back.

> Amanda and I pastor a healthy, growing church plant that, on paper, is what most church planters dream of.

A little backstory about Amanda and me: We pastor a healthy, growing church plant that, on paper, is what most church planters dream of. We saw significant growth in a short period of time in an uncommonly small and unconventional city called Branson, Missouri. Unfortunately, we planted our church without a network or support system and felt the pains of being orphans. We took initiative, self-taught ourselves, and grew despite the lack of mentors. At the time, I did not recognize that this had been a recurring theme for my entire life. With that said, the last thing I wanted was for another pastor to feel what we had felt. For this reason, I was excited to be a part of something like this!

I had been given the wonderful opportunity to meet Pastor Scott less than two years before this retreat and had built an extremely close bond. I had flown to Dallas multiple times to learn from him, spent time with his executive team, and allowed my team to learn from his staff. I was receiving the mentorship that I had craved for so many years. As our relationship grew, Scott began bringing me in to help sketch out what this network would look like and how we could help these church plants grow. I was on cloud nine listening to Andy lay out his plan for how we could plant and physically support hundreds of church plants. It was in those early days that the groundwork for the Father Initiative was born. So when Amanda and I went to the retreat, we were ready to hit the ground running.

Now, let's go back to that moment in the conference room. As we sat around a table with the other pastors, the retreat took a turn I had never expected. Pastor Scott started sharing what it means to be a father and how God's plan for us is to father sons, not just physically, but also spiritually. To be honest with you, this was not a surprise for Amanda and me as I had heard Scott share his heart on this matter more times than I can count! But what took place next, I had not anticipated. Pastor Scott and Jenni became very raw and shared many stories about their family of origin and how these areas played a role in their lives as adults. There were many tears as their stories were incredibly heartfelt. Then, Scott did the unthinkable. He asked us to share about our childhood and relationship with our parents.

For many people, this would not be a huge ordeal, but for me, this was the beginning of discovering years of hurt being buried or, as my therapist likes to say, protected by my conscious thoughts. Where I was sitting at the table, I would be the last to go. Pastor after pastor shared their stories. With every story being shared, it was like little openings of awareness in my life were torn open, until finally, I was flooded with emotions. Feelings and thoughts that I had no idea were there began to surface. By the time my turn came, I was swimming with emotions; it was hard to articulate how I was feeling, and all I could muster was, "I do not know how to be a father because I don't even know how to be a son." I was flooded with guilt; however, in most cases, this is misdirected. My mind felt tangled with confusion.

"I do not know how to be a father because I don't even know how to be a son."

How could I have parent issues? Of course, I realized that my childhood was far from "normal," and I understood that I was exposed to a lot of unhealthy things. However, I am successful, have a great marriage, parent good kids, pastor a wonderful church, and live financially stable. Doesn't that mean that I overcame all those issues in my past? Doesn't that mean I should not be feeling all these emotions? As my therapist would tell me months later, "Two things can be true at the same time." I can have a dysfunctional past that I never really dealt with, while at the same time, I have learned how to cope with the hurts in ways that have allowed me to be successful in many areas. The problem is that deep emotional wounds left unexposed do not just heal themselves, and over time they infect different areas of your life.

Based on Pastor Scott's example, I found myself pursuing therapy. I was thirty-six years old when I stepped into the therapist's office for the first time. I had no idea what to expect, just the realization that there were some things below the surface that I needed to discover. Just to clarify,

I knew there was dysfunction in my relationship with my parents, and I knew that my childhood was not healthy, but what I did not realize was the residual effects of those things that transpired in my adult life.

I was the oldest by five years to two other siblings who were a year apart. My mother struggled with mental challenges that she refused to accept, and my father, due to work, was only home four to five days a month. However, if he got into an argument with my mom, we might not have contact with him for several months. From a very young age, I took a lot of the responsibility in the home by completing chores, caring for my younger siblings, and mostly consoling my mother overwhelmed by her emotions due to her marriage, finances, and friendships.

Around the end of my fourth-grade year, I started to recognize that maybe my family wasn't exactly typical. This was now the sixth school I was beginning, and I realized that probably was not most children's experiences. I wish I could say this constant moving ended in fourth grade, but this was a continual theme from my childhood through high school graduation. We moved for many reasons, but the most recurring reason was that my mother would have an issue with a family member or coworker, or some financial mistake was made. When one of these issues would occur, we packed up everything and moved away from the so-called situation.

My mother tended to get manic in certain scenarios, and she had a tendency to believe she was always a victim. When a circumstance would arise, she truly believed that the other party involved was this person whose sole objective was to hurt her. In those situations, my mom was convinced that she was entirely innocent. Because of that, she would manipulate in her mind what had happened to fit the narrative that she believed or ultimately make something up. However, *she* was convinced that it was 100 percent true.

To put it simply, that was a lot to be exposed to as a child. As the oldest sibling in my family, it became my job to console with very little consoling being given to me. Because of these circumstances, as I grew older, I became calloused to my mother's stories. I started identifying the exaggerations and mistruths. Not only that, but I started viewing others and their hurts with an air of annoyance. My thought process was based on the idea that if I could make it out of my childhood, then I had no business crying about what I was going through. "Suck it up and get moving" was my motto! I found myself emotionally removed from everyone. I was strictly goal-oriented with my team and emotionally disconnected even from my own children.

"Suck it up and get moving" was my motto!

Of course, I did not recognize it until I opened the Pandora's box of my family of origin. It was through exposing my past that I can now put in the work to see my future painted in health. I can now confidently know that I am working hard to make sure that I can be a healthier father, husband, leader, pastor, and friend. I am far from perfect, but I have leaped light years beyond where I started. My goal is that as I unpack my story for you in a very vulnerable way, you will begin to understand that you, too, can discover that vulnerability is not weakness but immense strength. Through that strength, you can start walking towards who you are created to be, regardless of how you were raised!

As we go through this journey together, you may read my story and think, *My childhood was not that extreme.* In doing so, you may believe that because your childhood was not as intense as mine, that maybe your hurts are exaggerated. As my therapist says, "Not every family is dysfunctional; only dysfunctional families say that to downplay their dysfunction." However, just because not all families are dysfunctional, doesn't mean all families are perfect. With that said, as a child, the family in which you were raised was your entire world. In your childhood, you did not have the luxury of comparing your world against my world. What you experienced was defining for you and shaped you for better or worse. My prayer for you is that we expose some wounds that you may have hidden in your mind so that we can see them treated and turned into a testimony for good!

Unfortunately, self-evaluation is one area most people rarely participate in. To look inward is incredibly uncomfortable as no one wants to relive old hurts. Also, no one likes to admit there may be some negative behaviors, mindsets, or actions in our lives. However, left unaddressed, we could find ourselves in a place where we hurt our marriages, our team members, and sadly, our children! I heard a story once illustrating that you could go three weeks without brushing your teeth, and even though your nose is inches from your mouth, you could not tell your breath stinks; however, everyone else in the room with you could! Why? Because many of us are utterly oblivious to the harmful behaviors in our lives, even though they are apparent to everyone else.

As I was reflecting on that story, this thought came into my mind: *Though that illustration is true, we now have a situation where we may have experienced our bad breath in ways we might not have in the past.* Why do I say that? Because we have had to wear masks due to a pandemic. How many of you didn't realize you had some rough-smelling breath until you put that mask on? Why is that? Because when you put that mask on, you are redirecting your breath back to you. This is precisely what we have to learn to do as people in regards to our growth. We must redirect our behaviors, mindsets, and actions back towards ourselves to understand where we can move towards health.

Like it or not, we all develop coping mechanisms along the way to deal with our wounds. In that, we may have subconsciously learned how to protect ourselves so that we do not experience that wound again. The problem arises when we do not learn to cope in a healthy way or when we are oblivious to the emotional walls we put up to keep us, in our minds, safe. There is a testimony of redemption and healing in the story of your life. God can turn the pain you have experienced in this fallen world into good (Romans 8:28) if you are willing to submit yourself to the process of healing. I am excited to go on this journey with you!

There is a testimony of redemption and healing in the story of your life.

CHAPTER 3

WHY DO YOU NOT WANT ME?

From as far back as I can remember, it has been communicated to me that my father was not present for the first three years of my life. Not only was he not in my life, but he refused to believe that I was his son. He felt my mother must have gotten pregnant by someone else, while she insisted he was the father. Until I was three, it was just my mother and me; I did not personally remember these early years, but my mom would replay the story for me often. Why? It's difficult to comprehend why this was pertinent knowledge to share with a child with no previous recollection of his father's absence. However, it was communicated frequently.

My mother never spoke about my birth in a derogatory way; instead, it was always a flippant joke, a statement that was casually tossed around like a fun fact at a dinner party.

Not only was it a regular topic of conversation, the running joke was that both my siblings and I were accidents. More specifically, I was conveyed as a "pill baby" that just so happened to spring onto the scene unintentionally. My mother never spoke about this in a derogatory tone, but instead it was always a flippant joke, a statement that was casually tossed around like a fun fact at a dinner party. Hey, let's play two truths and a lie! Okay, I will go first. Michael's father did not claim him for the first three years of his life, we were happily married preparing to start a family, and Michael was an accident, more specifically, a "pill baby." Which is the lie? That was fun!

To be honest, I did not realize how much this had affected me throughout my entire life. In the last few years, I have had this deep desire to get a paternity test. Yet, in the same breath, I am also extremely scared to take one. I keep replaying all the scenarios in my head: *Is he my birth father? If not, that would explain a lot. Do I really want to find out the truth? Do I even want to discover if there is another person that could be my father? Am I just crazy to even have these doubts? My father and I do not look anything alike, and I don't look like my siblings. Am I just overthinking it?* I have gone back and forth with these thoughts in my mind. However, the real question at the root of it all is, "Why did you not want me?"

Why was I not good enough? Why was I an accident? And most importantly, why did you not fight for me? Every child desperately wants to know that he is worth fighting for. Every son wants to know that his dad would protect him at all costs. Yet, I have had this sinking feeling that nudges my mind with the thought that maybe my father did not have that desire.

As I grew older, the impact of my father's absence, which I mentioned in chapter one, started to take its toll. It is hard for a boy not to see his father very often when he is growing up. Now, I understood my father's need to provide for our family, and when he was home, he spent as much time as possible with us as children. I am glad that I had a father that did not ignore us as children so that he could enjoy his own activities instead.

The struggle for me was that my father knew about my mother's mental instabilities and the impact that it had on us as kids, but he did nothing to make our situation better. As I grew older, my mother's manic tendencies started to become directed toward me. However, no matter what I would express to my dad, all I would get was a passive response. He would mitigate my frustrations by saying, "You know how your mother is," or even worse, he would just change the subject. I did not need that! I needed a father to protect me!

I was the child left to defend myself. I was the child picking up the pieces of my mother's destruction and packing every U-Haul for every move absent of my father. Even to this day, my father would rather ignore than defend. "No confrontation" is my dad's motto, and still, my inner child pops out, "Why do you not want me? Why will you not fight for me?"

> I was the child left to defend myself. I was the child picking up the pieces of my mother's destruction and packing every U-Haul for every move absent of my father.

These are not questions a child should be left to answer on his own. Maybe my father did not know how to answer those questions for me because no one had ever answered them for him. The issue is not what my father did or did not do, but instead the impact his actions, or lack thereof, had on me as I went out into this world searching for those answers. Now that I am a father, how do I break this unhealthy chain for my children? At the core of who you are, healthy identity is everything, but we can never discover that identity apart from our Heavenly Father. However, if we are honest with ourselves, it is challenging to view God the Father through a separate lens from your earthly father. No matter how much we know, we still naturally drift toward what we have experienced from our past. For many years, this was me, and this unhealthy view of God the Father crippled me.

When you read through the Word of God, it is hard not to see the powerful illustrations of fatherhood. One of my favorite characters in Scripture is Jacob. Jacob had a troubled past that he overcame, which could be the theme of a book itself, but I want to highlight him more specifically as a father. See, Jacob was madly in love with Rachel, so much so that he worked for her father for seven years to earn the right to marry her. However, his ol' dad-in-law played a switch-a-roo on the wedding night and sent Rachel's older sister, Leah, into the tent to consummate the marriage. Talk about a surprise for Jacob the next morning! However, custom was custom, and the oldest daughter had to be married first, so Jacob ended up marrying both of them.

Now, of course, Jacob favored Rachel. Because of Leah's sadness, God allowed her to conceive first. Leah had six boys before Rachel had her first child. On top of that, two servants had four additional boys belonging to Jacob before Rachel gave birth to her son. When Rachel birthed her firstborn, Joseph, he was the apple of Jacob's eye. The Bible even goes as far as to say in Genesis 37:3, "Jacob loved Joseph more than any of his other children because Joseph had been born to him in his old age. So one day Jacob had a special gift made for Joseph—a beautiful robe." After this, the Bible says in verse 4, "But his brothers hated Joseph because their father loved him more than the rest of them. They couldn't say a kind word to him." They hated him because of how their father loved him, so they decided to get rid of Joseph. His brothers sold him into slavery and faked his death to explain to their dad what had happened to Joseph. How did Jacob respond to the news of his son's alleged death? The Bible says in verses 34 and 35, "Then Jacob tore his clothes and dressed himself in burlap. He mourned deeply for his son for a long time. His family all tried to comfort him, but he refused to be comforted." "I will go to my grave mourning for my son," I imagine he would say, and then he would weep.

Jacob was in deep mourning and turned his affection to Rachel's only other child, Benjamin. Years later, when Joseph, unbeknownst to his brothers, was second-in-command of Egypt, he required his brothers to bring back his little brother, Benjamin, when they returned to Egypt. Watch again Jacob's reply to his sons in Genesis 42:38 (emphasis added):

But Jacob replied, "My son will not go down with you. His brother Joseph is dead, and he is all I have left. If anything should happen to him on your journey, you would send this grieving, white-haired man to his grave."

As I read this story, I had two thoughts running through my head. *What would it feel like to be loved by a father that intensely?* What an amazing feeling to have a father grieve for you and long for you with such devotion! To know how special you are in your father's eyes must breathe so much confidence and security into your spirit. No wonder Joseph was faulted for bragging so carelessly about his dreams; no part of him questioned who he was in his father's eyes. However, I kept putting myself in his brothers' shoes. Maybe it was because those are shoes I had been accustomed to wearing. *How must they have felt to have their father publicly express how their younger brother Joseph was the one he loved more than them all?* Not only did he verbally express this, but he made Joseph a unique coat as a visible symbol that they were not as valuable in their father's eyes as Joseph was.

Then, years later, when confronted with the possibility that Benjamin had to go on this journey, Jacob had the gall to say, "He is all I have left." What do you mean he is all you have left? Of course, you do not want harm to come to Benjamin, but you still have ten older sons! How that must have stung in their hearts. After serving their father all these years, none of them had ever reached the level in Jacob's eyes of being enough. I wonder if these boys, probably like their mothers, asked themselves continuously, *Why do you not want me?*

I can tell you that not feeling wanted
or worthy of being fought for is one
of the most devastating conditions
that can manifest in a child's life.

I can tell you that not feeling wanted or worthy of being fought for is one of the most devastating conditions that can manifest in a child's life. You always walk around with this insecurity that you are not valuable and believe everyone will sooner or later discover how worthless you are. My father dealt with many insecurities of his own, and they manifested themselves in sarcasm and demeaning jokes. He would make fun of my physical appearance and say he wished he could change things about me that were physically impossible to change. He would harp on my failures in activities, and I would feel like there was no level of success I could ever achieve. It was all done in the vein of what he called humor, and unfortunately, my siblings and I were all targets of his cruel jokes.

Because of his example, my siblings and I joked harshly with each other as we were very mean with our words. Now I understand this was what my father received and how he coped with the insecurities he felt from his father never being present. The reality is that hurt people hurt people, and many times, the hurt is inflicted unintentionally. I do not believe with any part of me that my father's objective was to inflict wounds. That does not excuse his actions, but, it is a fact that when we live with untreated wounds, we have the capacity to hurt others through our pain, whether we mean to or not.

As a child growing up with those critical questions not being answered, I had the tendency to mask myself with a false sense of security. I acted like I was great, and nothing bothered me. However, deep down, I felt worthless. I had a hard time believing anybody wanted me in their life. I second-guessed my friends, girls I dated, and all adult figures. I felt like people put up with me, but they did not really want me in their life or even like me. This even translated to the way I felt about God. I mean, I had all the knowledge about what was right, but for some reason, I could not get what I knew in my head to penetrate my heart.

Do not get me wrong; these were not conscious decisions on my part. But as I reflect on my mentalities and actions, you can see my insecurities were the main characters in my story. I believed God forgave me, but I never felt special to Him. I knew God loved me, but it felt more like a requirement than a delight. I kept having this sinking feeling that God put up with me, so I was not even close to being a favorite to Him. I believed there were many more people that God would choose over me.

As I reflect on my mentalities and actions, you can see my insecurities were the main characters in my story.

This stayed with me through many, many years of ministry. I would teach people about God's love for them yet still question His love for me. I truly believed it was valid for them; I just felt like it was Jesus' interaction with God the Father on the day He was baptized. It was a story I have personally read more times than I can count, yet my heart was opened in a way it had never been towards a father. Matthew 3:17 records it as, "And a voice from heaven said, 'This is my Son, whom I love; with him I am well pleased.'"

→ This is my son speaks to Jesus' identity.
→ Whom I love shows God giving Jesus affection.
→ With him I am well pleased voices God affirming Jesus.

Notice that God says all three of these things *before* Jesus performed any miracles, preached any sermons, or did any public ministry. It was not what Jesus could do that pleased God as His Father, but who Jesus was. Pastor Scott went on to say there is a reason that this was shared in an audible voice. We need to hear these three things from our earthly fathers and our Heavenly Father.

Despite the pains from our childhood, we must grasp how God sees us. We are His children. Not only are we His children, but He has chosen to be a Father to us! He says, "And I will be your Father, and you will be my sons and daughters,' says the Lord Almighty" (2 Corinthians 6:18). Get that into your spirit! There is no point in the history of your life that God has or will deny that He is your Father. You are not an accident! Not only that, but you are also loved deeply by God, and nothing you could ever do could take away His love from you! The apostle Paul said,

> *And I am convinced that nothing can ever separate us from God's love. Neither death nor life, neither angels nor demons, neither our fears for today nor our worries about tomorrow—not even the powers of hell can separate us from God's love. No power in the sky above or in the earth below—indeed, nothing in all creation will ever be able to separate us from the love of God that is revealed in Christ Jesus our Lord.*
>
> —Romans 8:38-39

What makes these verses so powerful is that God is making it clear that there is nothing in the physical or spiritual realm that could take away the love your God has for you. Your God the Father wants you and profoundly loves you with a love that is humanly impossible to understand fully. Lastly, God the Father is pleased with you, not because of what you did or did not do, but because of who you are!

Sometimes we think we must earn God's love and approval because we feel we must do that with our earthly parents. Sometimes we think that we have screwed up so much that we must work hard to make up for our mistakes. We believe that maybe He could be pleased with us again over time. I think Paul said it perfectly in Romans 5:8, "But God showed His great love for us by sending Christ to die for us while we were still sinners." God loved us and sent Jesus to redeem us in the midst of our failures. I am sure glad God did not wait for me to get my act together before He sent Jesus to save me!

I want you to understand that sometimes allowing these truths to penetrate your heart takes time, and you may have to remind yourself of their validity regularly. Like Paul says in Colossians, we grow as we learn to know God better and better. That is precisely what we are going to do on this journey. We will discover our wounds and then discover God's truth, which is the only way to healing!

We will discover our wounds and then discover God's truth, which is the only way to healing!

CHAPTER 4

A MAN ALREADY?

John Eldredge's writings have this beautiful gift of resonating so profoundly with me as a person. I have read his books since college and reread them more times than I can count since then. In his book *Fathered by God*, John discussed the masculine journey that should unfold from Boyhood to Cowboy to Warrior to Lover to King to Sage. Eldredge believes that this is the healthy transition every boy *should* make. Unfortunately, very few of us travel down this path and navigate through these stages with a guide, a father, to show us the way. Whether this is a result of the fatherless generation that plagues our world or due to a father that was abusive, absent, or simply did not know how to help his child transition through these stages, many men have never experienced a father guiding them when growing up. John wrote in his book:

> *Great damage is done if we ask a boy to become a king too soon, as is the case when a father abandons his family, walking out the door with the parting words, "You're the man of the house now." A cruel thing to do, and an even more cruel thing to say, for the boy has not yet become a man, not yet learned the lessons of boyhood and then young manhood. He has not yet been a warrior, nor a lover, and he is in no way ready to become a king.*[2]

I cannot begin to express how the words that John penned years ago flooded my mind with memories of my childhood and pressed on the sensitive wounds of my soul. My father did not abandon our family in the exact way John described, but he was physically absent. My father

---

2   John Eldredge, *Fathered by God* (Nashville: Thomas Nelson, 2009).

didn't walk out on our family, but I remember very early on my dad looking at me, the oldest child, and saying, "You are the man of the house." Those words can be innocent when told in a manner to affirm his son where the father is gone for a weekend. However, they are incredibly damaging when the father is away from home more than he is present at home, and the responsibilities of the son are in alignment with the fact that he is the man of the house.

It was probably around second grade when my mom called me into the living room and told me to go outside and mow the grass. Not knowing anything about yard maintenance or even running a lawnmower, I headed out to hop on our "huge," late-eighties riding lawnmower. My mom showed me how to turn it on, start it, and stop it. Moments later, I was off to the races! I was flying around the yard, learning how to control the speed, taking turns too fast, and almost decapitating myself on the clothesline. However, to a second-grade boy, this was a blast! From that day forward, it was my job, a job that would become much less enjoyable as the years would go by.

Along with lawn maintenance, I would take on other chores and responsibilities around the home that my father was not present to do. There is nothing wrong with a child doing chores, but the damage came from the fact that there was an expectation that was put on me from a young age to fill a void that my father left behind. I did not learn the necessary skills or tasks next to my father but alone. I had to teach myself how to accomplish the tasks that were asked of me, which causes an immense amount of insecurity in a boy.

I had to teach myself how to accomplish the tasks that were asked of me, which causes an immense amount of insecurity in a boy.

Not only was there the expectation to fill those voids through chores, but there were emotional and relational voids that my mother insisted that I fill in her life. There were countless tear-filled conversations that I had with my mother from childhood into my teenage years. She expressed her grief over my father, the person at work that had wronged her, the family member we were now at odds with, and the countless financial struggles our family had. I became much more than a sounding board; I became her consoling companion. I would get angry at my father or those that I believed mistreated my mother. I would stress and fret over the finances. I thought my job as a child was to make my mother feel better. When my dad came home, I would let him have it. When my mom complained about others wronging her, I would come to her defense and tell her how horrible those people were and how right she was. When the finances were precarious, which was 90 percent of the time, I answered the phone to get rid of the bill collectors and help keep the financial mess hidden from my father.

Because of all this added responsibility that I inherited from my childhood, I grew up with this sense that the only person who could teach me life lessons was myself. I was highly independent and even felt this internal need that I must not need anyone. I had this mentality that I was smart enough and strong enough, and because of that, I could muster up the wisdom to progress in life. Unfortunately, a boy needs a father to guide him, and he needs a father to show him the way. John made a statement that honestly broke my orphan heart, "Masculinity is *bestowed*. A boy learns who he is and what he's made of from a man."

A boy travels through the stages of masculinity because a father or father figure passes on the knowledge and demonstrates what a child needs. I think back to my dad and how very non-confrontational he was with subjects that mattered. He had no fear to complain or say a demeaning joke, but when it came to serious matters, they were left to someone else. I remember when my mom nagged my dad to have the "talk" with me. He beat around the bush the entire conversation until finally, he said, "Michael, you can do everything else with a girl. Just do not have sex." First off, what is sex really, and secondly, is that really what you should tell a fifth grader? When my mom found out that my dad did not clarify anything, she decided to have the "talk" with me, and I can tell you from firsthand experience that is the last conversation you, as a fifth-grade boy, want to have with your mother! You do not even want to know the conversation Ole Dad had with me the night before my wedding!

I needed those conversations, and I needed that fatherly role model around. As I grew up, I never had that, and I did not realize how much of the father figure I was in the home. I remember when I was in my mid-twenties, my little brother got angry at me and started screaming, "You left me and never taught me how to be a man!" By leaving him, he was referencing the fact that I went to college and got married. Because our father was not present, to him, I was that figure. He did not yell those things at our dad, but instead he turned those words on me. Our dad was always gone, and I was the male role model present in his life. In his eyes, I had abandoned him because I moved on into adulthood. It was not right for my parents to put that weight on me, but it was also unfair that my dad was not there for my brother either. In fact, I agree with John that it was downright cruel.

As a result of my independent nature, I had no clue how to have a mentor in my life. I did not know how to ask for advice or help or (much less) receive affirmation.

As a result of my independent nature, I had no clue how to have a mentor in my life. I did not know how to ask for advice or help or (much less) receive affirmation. I learned how to solve problems on my own, and I let my success become my affirmation. That is a really lonely place to find yourself. Not only did I not know how to have a physical mentor in my life, but I was oblivious of how to invite God into my life in that way. I loved God, prayed, and read the Word, but I still mustered up all my success with my own two hands. Unfortunately, your own strength will only take you so far.

I remember reading the book *Building Below the Waterline* by Gordan MacDonald, a must-read if I say so myself, where he describes Moses' mindset as he lead the people of Israel through the wilderness. Moses was bearing the weight of a leadership position that was much greater than his talents would suggest he could handle. How he approached this season is so relevant for you and me. He lead a people group that was far from perfect, and despite all the miracles they saw God do, they still wandered towards their sinfulness.

So, in Exodus 33, the people of Israel were caught worshiping a man-made golden calf. Mind you, this was after they saw God deliver them from Egypt, part the Red Sea, and bring miraculous food and water; they still began worshiping a fake god. Why? Because to them, God was a distant figure. He had a relationship with Moses, but they saw that relationship from afar. So Moses' response was to build a prayer tent of sorts that was within eyeshot of the people. The Bible says that Moses would go into this tent, and the cloud of God's Spirit would hover at its entrance as the Lord spoke with Moses.

Watch how the people responded as this happened in verse 10, "When the people saw the cloud standing at the entrance of the tent, they would stand and bow down in front of their own tents." Moses, a father figure to these former slaves, modeled to them the intimacy with God. The Bible responds in verse 11, displaying that intimacy, "Inside the Tent of Meeting, the Lord would speak to Moses face-to-face, as one speaks to a friend."

While all this is incredibly powerful, the conversation that God and Moses had took it to another level. Moses understood that this task was physically impossible unless God the Father stepped in, so Moses prayed for three specific things.

MOSES PRAYED FOR GOD'S PRESENCE

One day Moses said to the Lord, "You have been telling me, 'Take these people up to the Promised Land.'" . . . Then Moses said, "If you don't personally go with us, don't make us leave this place."
—Exodus 33:12,15

Moses was telling God the Father, *I don't want Your promises without Your presence.* You have given me a mission, but I can't do it with talent, charisma, or knowledge alone. I need your presence. I need the people I lead to experience that You are with us always. You never leave us, and You will never forsake us. To be honest, this is precisely what a child longs for from his earthly father. I do not need the things you can buy as much as I just need you in my life. As I mature and navigate through the stages of life, I need the comfort that Dad will be there every step of the way. Your presence carries more value than your purchases.

Unfortunately, if we have grown up with a father that was not present through life's changes, it is easy to believe that God will be the same. We start feeling that God does not see us and that our prayers are not a priority to Him. Deep down, we believe that God does not value us. I can scream that this is the farthest thing from the truth, and I can quote you scripture after scripture where God speaks about how much He cares about you, but the reality is you have to accept that truth yourself. There is an honest evaluation that you must make on how you view God and how that applies in your relationship with Him. You must take those lies captive and make them submit to the truth, and you must recognize that God the Father will never leave you.

MOSES PRAYED FOR GOD'S DIRECTION AND PURPOSE

Moses prayed, "Let me know your ways so I may understand you more fully and continue to enjoy your favor" (Exodus 33:13).

As a small child, that father figure in your life is the smartest person in the world. They know every fact and every solution to all of life's problems. As a father, if you nurture that relationship with your child, the hope is that as the questions become more in-depth and as the problems get bigger, you will be the ear that their concerns land on. Unfortunately, if a father figure is not present or is dismissive as the child grows, children will not reach out when they need direction the most. If you are like I was for many years, not only will you not reach out to your father, but you will not reach out to any mentor. You will decide alone, problem-solve alone, and ultimately feel alone. Not only do you start to feel alone in your physical relationships, but, spiritually, you can feel like an orphan also. This mindset can cause you to believe that God has other children that are more important to Him. Do not waste your time reaching out to God; He will not respond. Just handle it yourself.

Based on Moses' previous request, his desperation would not allow him to lead without God being involved. He cried in Exodus 33:13 (NIV), "Teach me your ways" and then followed it up in verse 15 (author paraphrase) by saying, "If you do not go with me, I am not going." It is like Moses was crying out to God, "I want to be a father like you. I want to lead with a heart like yours." Just like a child close to his father learns his father's values, we must also learn God's character and nature. Just as a child wants to be just like his daddy when he grows up, we must crave to be imitators of Jesus as we continue to grow in our faith.

> Just as a child wants to be just like his daddy when he grows up, we must crave to be imitators of Jesus as we continue to grow in our faith.

God, teach me your ways and correct me when I am not walking in them just as a father corrects his child. That is precisely what the writer of Hebrews says:

> And have you forgotten the encouraging words God spoke to you as His children? He said, "My child, don't make light of the Lord's discipline and don't give up when He corrects you. For the Lord disciplines those He loves, and He punishes each one He accepts as His child."
>
> —Hebrews 12:5-6

MOSES PRAYED FOR GOD'S GLORY

Moses' last words in that chapter sealed the deal: "Please, show me Your glory" (Exodus 33:18, NKJV).

I don't know about you, but I thought my daddy was the strongest man in the world when I was a small child. He could hit the baseball and throw the football farther than anybody else. I loved watching him do all the things that left me in awe. That awe in your father causes you to run to him when you are scared, stand behind him when you need protection, and seek him when you need help. If that relationship is nurtured as you grow, that awe turns into a genuine respect, and that is the foundation of a trusting relationship. No matter what I face in this life, it will not defeat me if my daddy is present!

Your Father God wants to be awe-inspiring in your life. He wants to display His glory and grandeur to you, but He will never force Himself into your life. He is on the edge of His throne waiting for you to call out to Him, and you better believe He is willing to show up in miraculous ways. All you have to do is open up your life to Him. You do not have to do the miracle yourself, you do not have to display all your greatness, and you do not have to carry that weight with your own strength. You are not called to be the Savior. Invite God the Father in, and remember He never leaves you, He wants to be a voice in your life, and He wants to do the impossible!

Gordon MacDonald posed Moses' mindset in a powerful yet so simple prayer that goes, "Teach me your ways, guarantee me your presence, and show me your glory all the days of my life." What a beautiful way to step into each day, inviting God into our lives and submitting to Him as our Father.

CHAPTER 5

AM I GOOD ENOUGH?

I can still feel the knots in my stomach, the anxiousness that gripped me the night before attending a new school. This was not a once or twice occurrence in my life but something I would repeat twelve different times. I remember lying in bed, not being able to sleep with so much fear running through my mind. Where will I sit at lunch? This is probably the root of some of the deepest anxiety for a new kid at school. The uncertainty of standing in the middle of an unfamiliar lunchroom filled with kids who already know which table their friends will be eating at can be extremely scary. When I find a seat, will it be like Forrest Gump on the bus: "Can't sit here"?

Then, there was the added pressure that now I would have a whole new set of kids I must impress and hope some of them will like me enough to call me their friend. That becomes much more challenging as you become a teenager since friend groups and best friends are pretty established. I always had this thought running through my mind that none of the kids wanted me around and that many of them just put up with me. I felt like a little brother just following his older brother around everywhere he went. In desperate need of being accepted into a new environment, I would become a chameleon. I would figure out what I believed that friend group would want, and then I'd overcompensate in a big way. In some schools, I would be the class clown; in other schools, I was the rebellious daredevil, or the tough guy, or the rich kid (which was the farthest thing from the truth, but I did have a pretty good shoe game). At some schools, I acted like I was a ladies' man that never feared rejection. These identities were laced with insecurity and deep fear that I would be discovered as a fraud, and deep down, I never believed anyone would like me for me.

I felt like a little brother just following his older brother around everywhere he went.

There were times when my plan worked, and other times I had to pivot in a big way. I remember one of my most utter failures came in the eighth grade. It was the third day of a new school, and I played the rich/cool kid card. I decided to wear a fresh pair of the Air Penny 1s and a cool matching Nike T. Now, all of that was on point, but it took a wrong turn with the jeans I decided to wear. I was wearing some light-washed jeans ripped up, but I still passed the mirror check with flying colors, and off I went to dominate this new school. This story takes a dark turn during science class. I was sitting front row at one of the lab tables. I noticed many kids giggling in class, and kids kept coming up front to throw garbage away as they started busting out laughing. I had no clue what was so funny, but I was doing a Joey from *Friends* giggle to act like I knew what was going on. Then I made the worst decision ever as I turned sideways in my seat. The boy across from me made eye contact, looked down at my crotch, and his face turned white. All of a sudden, dread filled every part of my being as I knew the laughter must be directed at me. I looked down, and to my horror, one of the tears in my jeans and a shift in boxers now positioned themselves in perfect alignment for my humiliation. It was like a solar eclipse, a rare alignment, that if looked at without proper protection, would cause a blinding effect. I decided on day three of a new school to expose myself to my entire eighth-grade science class!

Albeit a very true story that I wish were not, it is an exaggerated reference to my point. I desperately wanted to be seen as enough to people; it was exhausting as a child to have to start all over again continually. This is probably why I crave words of affirmation so much as an adult because I always doubted that I was good enough growing up. I wish I could say that though navigating through new schools was difficult,

I did not face those insecurities in my home. Unfortunately, we did not have a very affirming household, as I referred to earlier. We threw insults at each other daily and a compliment was unheard of in our home. We learned from Dad that no one was off-limits. He would criticize my mom's weight in front of us and make jokes about her appearance. He would make fun of each of us and our physical imperfections. He had a remarkable talent of watching you play sports or participate in an activity and giving you a long list of everything you did wrong, yet never communicate what you did right. So, of course, as children, we lived what we learned. We were horrible towards each other as siblings. I have watched old home movies of my siblings and me, and I am appalled at how we talked to each other. I would be devastated if my kids said those things to each other. We made fun of my dad and my mother, and we would never in a million years allow a nice comment to cross our lips.

Not only did this cause us to be extremely hurtful towards each other, but it also made me deeply insecure. I wish this were something that I naturally grew out of. Unfortunately, as I have aged, my hurtful words have continued to journey with me. They have matured as they have packaged themselves in inconspicuous ways to conceal the bluntness of their intent. No longer would I hurl an obscene string of insults that were immediately seen as name-calling. I now introduced my negativity with its not-so-distant cousin, sarcasm. I used to brag about how my love language was sarcasm. Everything was packaged as me just joking around. In reality, I was hurting many people when I would insult traits I disliked about their lives. I wish I could say that is far behind me, but I occasionally catch myself laughing at someone else's expense even to this day.

The truth is that anytime you criticize, insult, or demean someone, it is rooted in your own insecurities. Deep down, we are just trying to make ourselves feel better about who we are, and our flesh's response is to make someone else feel worse about themselves. Our sinful nature convinces our subconscious that if we can make someone else be perceived as smaller, we will be perceived as more significant. I say your subconscious because that is exactly what it is. Very rarely is someone consciously aware of hurting another person that way. What typically occurs is that our defense mechanisms kick in without our conscious recognizing it, and we react. We must recognize unhealthy behaviors and understand the deep needs that must be filled for every child of God.

The truth is that anytime you criticize, insult, or demean someone, it is rooted in your own insecurities.

Insecurities and unfulfillment are rooted in a lack of identity. How can Paul say in Philippians 4:11-13:

> *Not that I was ever in need, for I have learned how to be content with whatever I have. I know how to live on almost nothing or with everything. I have learned the secret of living in every situation, whether it is with a full stomach or empty, with plenty or little. For I can do everything through Christ, who gives me strength.*

Now I get it. You will read this, and the obvious answer is that Paul can say that because Jesus gives us strength, but how many times do you think that is just a cliché church answer? I know you are raising your hand right now! How do we experience the strength that comes from Jesus? That is the question that we need answered. Well, look at what Paul says in verse 4 right before the passage we just read. "Always be full of joy in the Lord. I say it again—rejoice!" Do you see what Paul was saying here? He was saying there is a conscious decision to be filled with joy and rejoice, and it is found in Jesus. This is why he went on to say we are not to worry about anything. God's peace will guard your heart, and, there, you can be content in any situation. (I recommend reading the whole chapter yourself.) You may still think I am beating around the bush, but stay with me.

Paul learned the power of tying his identity to the will of God for his life. He discovered this tremendous understanding that he was not called to be anyone but Paul from Tarsus. He was not called to be Peter, Barnabas, Apollos, or the super-apostles he described in 2 Corinthians. Paul understood that despite what he was going through or where he was, the most incredible place of fulfillment and joy was found in accepting God's personal call for his life. That is why he could proclaim boldly, "Obviously, I'm not trying to win the approval of people, but of God. If pleasing people were my goal, I would not be Christ's servant" (Galatians 1:10).

If I am honest with myself, this has been a difficult lesson for me to understand and even more difficult for me to live. In my insecurity, I deeply strive for people's approval, and because of that, I constantly compare myself to others. Unfortunately, too many times, I think my value is found when I am perceived as better than others instead of when I am faithful to God and His call on my life. Too many of us have the wrong definition of success, and it is destroying our vision, our confidence, and most importantly, our identity.

The world's metrics for success tend to be based on statistics and comparisons. Let me pull out my stats and compare them to your stats. If my stats are better, than I am better than you, and if my stats are worse than yours, than I am less. Simply put, if my business has more sales than yours, naturally, my organization is better than yours. Of course, we know there are more in-depth metrics to measure an organization's health. Still, the premise is based on how we view ourselves, and as we live in a highlight-driven social media world, we most definitely subject our self-worth to that simplistic analysis.

Now, let's look at Heaven's metrics for success, which are based on stewardship and impact. Am I stewarding what I have been given by giving my absolute best, and am I making a difference through that stewardship? Do you see the difference here? No longer am I attaching my self-worth to what someone else does, but I am looking at the opportunities that I have been given and evaluating my stewardship level based on those opportunities. You have no authority in what other people do, but you do have a say in your own life. Once you grasp that, you quit letting other organizations and leaders have a say in your self-worth!

An excellent example of this is found in the parable Jesus tells about the servants with the talents found in Matthew 25. If you grew up in church for any length of time, this is a story that you have heard, but to be safe, let me paraphrase. A master was leaving town and called three of his servants to come to him so that he could entrust them with his wealth. He gave one servant five talents (a form of currency), another two talents, and the third servant one talent. Both the servant with five talents and the servant with two talents invested the money and doubled their investment. The servant with one talent was so fearful he would lose the one talent that he buried it until the master returned. When the master returned, he celebrated the servants who doubled their investments, but he cursed the fearful servant who buried the one talent. The moral of the story is to steward what you have been entrusted with as that pleases God. While that is most certainly true, there is a much more profound lesson to learn here.

Whenever we hear this parable, we tend to focus on the servant with one talent and the servant with five. We talk about how the servant with five trusted God, got to work, and doubled what he was given. What a fantastic guy! Next, we focus on the servant with one who was fearful, had no faith, and buried his treasure. What a letdown! The individual that we continuously ignore is the servant with two talents.

Let's quickly break this down. The servant with one talent basically looked at what he was given and thought to himself, *I do not have enough to do anything significant, so I am better off just settling with what I have and burying it, so at least I do not end up worse off than I already am.* The servant with two talents, who only had one more than the servant who believed he did not have enough to do anything significant, took what he was given and stewarded it to the point that it was multiplied. Now, get this. Even after he multiplied his treasure, he did not have as much as what the servant with five started with before he started investing. Yet, the master looked at them both and gave them the exact same praise. Why? Because the master was not concerned with the statistics as much as he was concerned with the stewardship!

Statistics never tell the whole story.

Statistics never tell the whole story. If all you do is look at statistics on a page, you miss all variables that go into those numbers. If you are a real estate agent and sell x amount a year and you look at a real estate agent from a different area who sells less than you, are you a better agent? Well, based on statistics, the answer is yes. However, there are many nuances to stats, and if you are a sports fan, you know this. How many times have you heard it said that the stats tell a different story than what actually happened in the game? Maybe some of the stats were garbage stats because of a blowout, or perhaps the athlete contributed in ways that cannot be seen in a stat sheet.

Let's go back to the real estate agents. Maybe the agent that sold more lives in a large metro area where house prices are considerably higher, and though they sold more in dollar amounts, they are a small fish in a large pond. Maybe the agent who sold less lives in a rural area or a smaller city with lower house prices. Even though they sold less in dollar amounts, they were in the top three agents in their area. This is the story of the talents. It is not the amount that matters, but the stewardship. However, much of our insecurity is rooted in our comparisons.

Some of us need to understand that we may never be the servant with five talents, which is completely fine. Just by me saying that, some people will be insulted by referencing the fact that they may be two-talent leaders. Why? Because again, our identity, which is our security and ultimately our joy, is not how God views us, but how others view us. Will you be fine if you do the planting and someone who waters sees the growth that God does? Will you be okay if you never have statistics that measure up to the "competition" you continuously compare yourself to? Will you be okay if the reward you get is found in Heaven? You will never rise above your insecurity and find fulfillment apart from the understanding that the greatest reward is, "Well done, my good and faithful servant," from a loving God who is proud of your stewardship. You are enough to Him!

CHAPTER 6

CAN I REALLY CHANGE?

As I mentioned earlier, I was quite the chameleon at every school I attended, doing my best to fit in and impress a new group of friends. I remember I moved to a new school with a month left of my fourth-grade year and, to my luck, attended the same school through my sixth-grade year. To fit in here, though, the other kids liked it when I was the class clown with a reckless side to me. I would get substitutes riled up by acting out and making the whole class crack up. I would not back down from any challenge another student presented me with. You dare it, and Michael will do it. This also got me into my fair share of fights.

However, something happened in my sixth-grade year that changed everything for me. My parents started to attend church when I was in fifth grade, which I didn't mind. I would attend and hang out with the kids at church. But in sixth grade, Jesus got a hold of my heart, and I decided to accept Him into my life. I got baptized that year, started getting involved in church programs, and was filled with the Holy Spirit. Needless to say, my life was changing! It also influenced the way I behaved at school towards the end of that year. I was no longer getting into fights, acting up in class, or getting sent to the principal's office. I was a new person, or so I thought.

There was less than a month left of my sixth-grade year, and my class was getting excited about summer and going to the junior high building for seventh grade. Randomly, my name was called over the intercom to come to the office. Not thinking anything of it, I was excused from class and made my way to the office. As I entered, the secretary said that the principal wanted to see me. Immediately, my mind started racing.

Why would he want to see me? I couldn't think of anything I had done wrong, so I decided it must not be a big deal.

As I entered his office, I noticed the junior high principal sitting in the office with him. My principal instructed me to sit down and then looked at the junior high principal and said, "Now this is the one that you are going to have to keep your eye on next year." I sat there panicking, not knowing what was going on. My principal continued, "He is nothing but a little troublemaker, and not only that, he is also a liar." I sank low in my chair, and my heart hurt so badly. He looked at me and projected, "You are a liar, aren't you, Michael?" In my mind, I was screaming, *NO! I am not a liar!* But shame and fear started to overwhelm me. With my head low, I replied, "Yeah, I am a liar." He then got what he wanted and dismissed me without another word.

I left the office feeling so defeated and overcome with shame. In my sixth-grade mind, I felt that he was an adult, so he must be right. I was the troublemaker and a liar. I could not change. Who I was is who I would always be. That is a lot to process for a child, and it shows how our words have authority and power. The sad part is that I told no one. I did not go home and communicate what happened to my mom; I did not call my dad or even address it with my teacher. I took it on the chin and dealt with the pain myself.

The sad part is that I told no one. I did not go home and communicate what happened to my mom; I did not call my dad or even address it with my teacher. I took it on the chin and dealt with the pain myself.

I had many ups and downs in my faith from that point on; of course, they were not all my former principal's fault, but that was a shift in my understanding of grace and forgiveness. I started to doubt that true forgiveness meant that we are new creations and thought more that we are just pardoned. I began to believe that God may forgive, but He does not forget.

If we are honest with ourselves, God's complete forgiveness is easier to *know* than to believe. That God, indeed, remembers our sins no more, as Hebrews 8:12 states, is hard for our human minds to wrap around. We may forgive someone, but how many of you know that offense is still tucked away nice and neat in the back of your mind? Not remembering almost feels impossible. Then, to believe that they can actually be a new creation ... what?!? People may get better, but new creations—like what they did never happened? No, that seems impossible, and to our worldly viewpoint, it is. However, aren't you glad we are citizens of Heaven, not this world? It is hard to view others through the heavenly lens of grace. It is also equally challenging to view ourselves through that lens.

Think about the life of Paul. There is a reason he stated:

> *Christ Jesus came into the world to save sinners—and I am the worst of them all. But God had mercy on me so that Christ Jesus could use me as a prime example of his great patience with even the worst sinners. Then others will realize that they, too, can believe in him and receive eternal life.*
> —1 Timothy 1:15-16

Before Paul's encounter with Jesus on the road to Damascus, he lived up to the moniker he gave himself in 1 Timothy as the worst of sinners. He was a religious zealot who had a deep hatred for the followers of Jesus, and that hatred fueled his sinful conquest to destroy Christians. Paul believed the lie that he was defending God while on his murderous rampage to eliminate the movement of Jesus at all costs. Not only was that his objective, but he had succeeded at murdering and arresting many Christians. So there was physical blood on his hands, and he had no plans of slowing down until the movement ended.

Yet, despite his immense sin, Paul (who at the time was referred to as Saul) encountered Jesus as a glorious bright light shining in the night, and Jesus' words pierced through, "Saul! Saul! Why are you persecuting me?" (Acts 9:4) I mean, of all the people, why would Jesus pick this murderer? I am sure He could have chosen someone with a better past. God knew everything Paul had done, and God was not confused when He approached Paul. In his book on Paul's life, Charles Swindoll referenced this moment and the depths of God's grace as this:

> We live in a culture that confuses humanity with deity. The lines get blurred. It's kind of sloppy theology that suggests God sits on the edge of Heaven thinking, Wonder what they'll do next? How absurd! God is omniscient. That implies, clearly, God never learns anything, our sinful decisions and evil deeds notwithstanding. Nothing ever surprises Him. From the moment we're conceived to the moment we die, we remain safely within the frame of His watchful gaze as well as His sovereign plan.

WOW! God knew every detail about Paul's sin, and still, He forgave him.

WOW! God knew every detail about Paul's sin, and still, He forgave him.

However, even after Paul's conversion, the followers of Jesus were very leery of Paul. Watch what happened a few verses later: "When

Saul arrived in Jerusalem, he tried to meet with the believers, but they were all afraid of him. They did not believe he had truly become a believer!" (Acts 9:26) Yet, Barnabas went around vouching for Paul and sharing with all about Paul's encounter with Jesus. Not only did he stay with the apostles, but Acts says he started preaching boldly about Jesus to the point where now the Jewish religious zealots wanted to murder him. Talk about a 180-degree change, from the hunter to the hunted.

With all that said, if someone who has a past that includes a murdering spree to wipe out Christianity (like Paul) can be radically changed, why is it so difficult to realize our past has been totally forgiven? I do not mean that your sins are covered up or excused enough so you can make it to Heaven. I mean, you were stained with filth, and now you are as white as snow. You are pure in the eyes of God because you received the forgiveness of Jesus that was paid for by His death and resurrection!

So how do you learn to walk in the fullness of that promise? The first thing you must develop is a mindset that says, "I will leave the past in the past!" Paul so pointedly stated:

> *I press on to possess that perfection for which Christ Jesus first possessed me. No, dear brothers and sisters, I have not achieved it but I focus on this one thing: Forgetting the past and looking forward to what lies ahead.*
> —Philippians 3:12-13

Paul knew he was not perfect, and he was not ignoring his mistakes, but he also knew where he was going. To get there, he had to look forward to what was ahead. Jesus instructed one of His followers with that same message when He said, "Anyone who puts a hand to the plow and then looks back is not fit for the Kingdom of God" (Luke 9:62).

Too many of us want freedom without releasing our past to Jesus.

You can't expect to walk in your complete God-given identity if you keep reliving your old life. The same way you will drift off course while plowing, you will drift off course in life. Too many of us want freedom without releasing our past to Jesus. We are chained to the past, and it keeps us from moving forward in life. It keeps us from progressing because we won't let go. We refuse to cut out the unhealthy things in our lives, and then we get deceived at times because we get a little slack in the chain. We think we have freedom because there is no tension at the moment, but that chain gets taut and pulls you back sooner or later. This is why James said:

> But when you ask him, be sure that your faith is in God. Do not waver, for a person with divided loyalty is as unsettled as a wave of the sea that is blown and tossed by the wind. Such people should not expect to receive anything from the Lord. Their loyalty is divided between God and the world, and they are unstable in everything they do."
>
> —James 1:6-8.

You can't walk in freedom while at the same time being unstable. You can't experience the fulfillment of your God-given identity while you still have a foot in your old life and this world.

Oftentimes, that is why Christians feel like they are not walking in the promises of God. It is not because God refuses to give the promises to them. On the contrary, it is because they keep looking back instead of forward. So let us look at three choices we need to make in order to press on to choose life and commit fully to God. And we must remember that making these decisions is a choice. Moses told the people of Israel:

> *"Today, I have given you the choice between life and death, between blessings and curses. Now I call on heaven and earth to witness the choice you make. Oh, that you would choose life, so that you and your descendants might live! You can make this choice by loving the lord your God, obeying him, and committing yourself firmly to him. This is the key to your life."*
>
> —Deuteronomy 30:19-20

INVITE THE HOLY SPIRIT TO SHOW YOU

There are lies we believe that we do not even realize are lies. We have been manipulated, have heard negative words spoken over us, or have internally accepted our self-deprecating thoughts to the point we have taken them as truth. Because of this, there are actions we are participating in or behaviors we have adopted that are contrary to our created identity. We must invite the Holy Spirit to expose the lies we believe and show us the truth.

The Bible says, "Satan, who is the god [notice it is a little "g" because he is a poser] of this world, has blinded the minds of those who don't believe. They are unable to see the glorious light of the Good News" (2 Corinthians 4:4). Not only does the devil work to blind those that are not followers of Jesus, but he wants to manipulate and blind the eyes of Jesus' followers as well. Just look at his manipulation of Adam and Eve. The devil loves for you to believe the lies and walk away from the truth—to forsake your identity and accept the falsehoods this sinful world has presented you with.

We need to recognize the enemy's motives and be conscious of God's desires for us. However, as we said earlier, the life God has for us is a choice, and God will never force Himself into your life. We have to decide to invite God into our lives just like David did in Psalms:

*Search me, O God, and know my heart; test me and know my
anxious thoughts. Point out anything in me that offends you, and
lead me along the path of everlasting life."*

—Psalm 139:23-24

I cannot say that this process is comfortable or enjoyable in the moment,
but I can promise you the freedom you feel later on in the process is
so liberating. As God starts pointing out these offenses and you start
giving them to Jesus, the weight of your past starts to leave, and the
freedom of your present and future begins to take over.

INVITE THE HOLY SPIRIT TO CHANGE YOU

The reason why so many of us attach ourselves to our past and never let
go is because that is all we know. Who are we without those behaviors,
mindsets, environments, or motivations? We have spent our whole
life putting up walls to protect ourselves, and the thought of being
vulnerable and exposing who we genuinely are is terrifying. However,
sin has a sick way of cozying up to our lives and telling us that this is
just who we are. That is just your personality, that is just the way you
were raised, no one is perfect, and the lies go on and on.

Sin is like a tumor; it attaches itself to your body and tells your brain
it is a part of you, and your brain believes it. That is why it does not
fight back. However, if that tumor is allowed to grow, it will cause dis-
figuration and even death. The only way to combat a tumor is through
surgery which is painful in the moment but saves your life in the long
run. There are things in our lives that must be removed because they
are killing who we are, and God is the only one who can remove them.
James very pointedly stated, "When sin is allowed to grow, it gives
birth to death" (James 1:15). There will be a lot of work to deal with
unhealthy habits that you have spent a lifetime establishing, and it will
not be comfortable addressing those wrong mindsets. Still, I am glad
our Jesus is willing to get uncomfortable with our mess. He is ready to
carry our burdens and give us His freedom.

> Sin is like a tumor; it attaches itself to your body and tells your brain it is a part of you, and your brain believes it. That is why it does not fight back.

The reality is that you may have these lingering thoughts that creep in asking whether Jesus can accept you. You may have doubts that you can change and question whether God wants to see you transformed. But I want you to remember David and listen to him after he committed the grave sin of adultery with Bathsheba, followed by having her husband murdered, "Create in me a clean heart, O God. Renew a loyal spirit within me" (Psalms 51:10).

You know what? Because of David's humble posture, God responded to his prayers. David did not end his life groveling in his past. He ended his life praising God for His mercy. David's family line became the fulfillment of the Savior's prophecy as David's became the lineage that Jesus came from. There is a legacy that you must choose to receive, and there is freedom from all your past hurts that you can receive. They are gifts that Jesus wants to give you freely. I hope you choose life!

INVITE THE HOLY SPIRIT TO FILL YOU

Trust me, Paul was not lying when He said, "It is more blessed to give than to receive" (Acts 20:35). I know, sometimes, we think change, giving Jesus our whole lives, and leaving the familiarity of our past are such enormous sacrifices, but I promise that you cannot outgive God. It is not a sacrifice if you get in return more than you gave.

Paul wrote to the Ephesian church and provided this instruction, "Don't be drunk with wine, because that will ruin your life. Instead, be filled with the Holy Spirit" (Ephesians 5:18). Paul was not focusing solely on being drunk from alcohol, but what the verse is saying is to stop self-medicating by using the things of this world. Quit trying to fill those hurts, voids, or insecurities with temporary comforts, and let the Holy Spirit in. Invite the Holy Spirit to be the Lord of your life as you surrender your mind and its thoughts, your ears and what they hear, your eyes and what they see, your mouth and what it says, your heart and its passions, your hands and what they strive to build, and your feet and what direction you go in life.

There is a reason why Jesus said it was better that He should go, so we could receive the Holy Spirit. Jesus told us what the Holy Spirit would be to us: "But the Helper [Comforter, Advocate, Intercessor—Counselor, Strengthener, Standby], the Holy Spirit, whom the Father will send in My name" (John 14:26). We cannot get enough of that in our lives. So daily, invite the Holy Spirit in, submit to His leading, and surrender to His authority, and watch how He gives you much more than you initially gave!

CHAPTER 7

WHOM CAN I TRUST?

"You were abused as a child." Those were the words that my therapist spoke to me that were ringing in my ears for weeks. Abused? It was hard for me to wrap my mind around that statement as I had never told myself that I was abused in all my years. But as I journeyed through therapy, more and more memories were unfolding. My therapist's statement came on the heels of several flashbacks that became apparent to me as I coached some pastors through their journeys. We were discussing why it is difficult as leaders to embrace a mentor fully. Many leaders can find it challenging to reach out and ask for advice. This can be for a litany of reasons. They could be insecure and fear their mentors will not think highly of them if they have struggles. Maybe they are scared to be a burden, or perhaps they have no idea how to invite someone into their lives. I tend to find that I am the latter.

As I was in this coaching session, my mind started racing as I asked myself why I was this way. Why is it so difficult to reach out and ask for advice and input? Why do I just bear the weight of every challenge on my own? Why am I so darn independent when I have so many willing mentors in my life? It is all rooted in the fact that I struggle with trust, and because I do not trust, my natural instinct is to protect myself, fend for myself, and depend only on myself. However, this is not a mindset that you are born with, so I started wrestling with why I would feel this way. As my therapist and I processed through years of pain, a Pandora's box of memories opened up leading to many tears.

As I mentioned earlier, when I was growing up, my mom struggled with mental illness. This caused her to live constantly in a victim state. She always had a villain to fight, and she was always wronged. My mom would concoct these elaborate stories, and she would believe they were true. As I started to mature, I began to connect the dots that no matter where we lived and my mother's situation, it would always end poorly, with my mom claiming to be mistreated. The common denominator was my mother, and as I got older, I started to recognize that the whole world could not be evil. Not every employer, family member, or friend had some dark motive to destroy her. As I started to understand that, the less I fed her pity. The less I consoled her, the more she turned her accusations on me. I felt as if I were in a constant state of defending myself from my mother's embellishments, and being the oldest sibling with my father never home, I was fighting this battle alone.

I felt as if I were fighting this battle alone.

It felt like everything came to a head the summer before my senior year in high school. This was when my mom began kicking me out of the home. As my mom's emotions receded, she would decide that she wanted me to come back. This started a roller coaster of being in and out of her good graces. I never knew which reaction I would get, so there was a constant state of tension.

Apparently, during this time, my father was getting a healthy dose of stories about me told to him by my mother. I remember the fall of my senior year coming home after I got off work at Long John Silvers and walking into the house. This was one of the rare times my dad happened to be home. He was agitated, and as I was walking to my room to get changed, he yelled, "Don't you have an attitude with me!" and charged into my room. To this day, I do not know what I did, but he got in my face screaming and started to head-butt me over and over.

I ran out of my room, heading to the front door, when he grabbed me and pushed me into the corner. He started to scream, "You think you are a man? I will show you who a man is!" and he began to punch me. At this time, I was on the floor, and all I could do was kick him off of me. Apparently, I kicked him in the groin. I ran to my car and drove to my work. I was bleeding from my nose and lip and had choke marks around my neck. My manager agreed that I needed to call the cops. An hour or so later, I got a call from a police officer. He had spoken with my parents and my siblings, who were in elementary school and not present for the incident. He said that I needed to quit exaggerating my story and that it sounded more like I attacked my father, not the other way around. No one came to look at my wounds or believed my story. Whom in authority can I trust?

Several months later, I was back home again, and my mother became upset and kicked me out of the home. So I moved in with some friends for what felt like the fifth or sixth time in several months. Again, my mom decided that I needed to come back home, and this time I refused. My mother scheduled a meeting with my principal to inform him that I lived out of the district. The only place I could find to live at seventeen years old was at my twenty-two and twenty-four-year-old friends' house. I slept on a twin bed that was shoved next to their washer and dryer in the laundry room that didn't have a door. I explained to my principal that our home was dysfunctional, how I never missed a day of school, that all my grades were As and Bs, and that I worked every day. He still told me that if I did not move back into the district, he would force me to transfer despite it being my senior year. Whom in authority can I trust?

So I moved back home, and about a month later, my mother was throwing my clothes in the front yard, kicking me out again. As I was loading up my car again, my mother informed me that I could not take the car. Now, mind you, this was the car that I had put the down payment on and paid for each monthly. However, because I was seventeen, the loan was in my father's name. Despite what she told me, I drove off in the car. That night, my friends and I were pulled over and surrounded by what felt like ten cop cars. I was taken out of the vehicle with guns drawn and thrown on the ground and arrested. I was taken to be charged as an adult and later discovered I was accused of two felony counts of grand theft auto and assault with a deadly weapon. My mother had also told the police that I tried to run her over.

I was stuck in a tiny jail cell with three other guys in their thirties and felt scared out of my mind. The following day a prosecuting attorney told me that I better write out a confession, or I would spend a minimum of five to seven years in prison. Luckily, I had enough sense not to do that as I knew I had every canceled check to show that I paid for my car. After a day or so, I believe my father told my mother to drop the charges. Whom in authority can I trust?

"Whom can I trust?" The answer that I gave myself for many years was "no one."

"Whom can I trust?" That has been a statement I have carried with me for many years into my adult life. The answer that I gave myself for many years was "no one." That was the motto I framed my life with. It was not something that I verbally said out loud or even a statement that I consciously understood, but it was the mindset that took root in my heart. There were no mentors I ran to for advice or any favors that I called in. I did not look to anyone to give me a shot or even believed anyone would actually want to help me in life. I was solely independent. The only one I could trust and count on was me. Not only did I not reach out to anyone for those things, but I believed if I did, those "people" that I sought out would either fail me or dismiss me. That was my only experience up to that point. Walls were formed in my life to protect me, and I always looked at people with a jaded perspective and kept them at arm's length.

It is funny how easily, as adults, we dismiss the struggles of young people as we will say things like, "You do not know what real stress is," or "Wait until you have the challenges we adults have." When we are honest and start diving into the pain we feel in adulthood, it is usually tied to the wounds we experienced in our childhood. It is easy to look at others when they are struggling and state with a condescending tone, "Get over it," "Grow up," or "You did not have a childhood as dysfunctional as mine." However, that is usually the response of someone who has not investigated the framing of his personality and character that was shaped through his formative years. We learn as children through our experiences how to survive in this world.

As a child, your home life is your entire world, and you learn how to survive. Of course, not every home is dysfunctional, but in the same sentiment, no home is perfect. Your parents are just trying to raise you based on what they know through what they have experienced. That is not an excuse for abuse and most certainly not an excuse for them to think they cannot work on their weaknesses. Yet, unfortunately, those excuses are where most people reside. I know I did for many years, and for many years I never understood why I reacted in specific ways and why it was so hard for me to let people in.

It is quite interesting how many skeletons you find in the closet of your mind when you decide, through therapy, to start exploring your childhood. However, I am consoled by the fact that first, I am not the only one that has pain in my past, and secondly, my past does not have to define my future if I address it and allow God to heal it.

When I was at this raw place of recognizing all the backstory of why I struggle with trust, God used my pastor, Scott Wilson, to speak into me. Scott was sharing about David's journey; I cannot tell you how much his story resonated with mine. David shared this very raw prayer in Psalms when he said, "Though my father and mother forsake me, the Lord will receive me" (Psalm 27:10, NIV). His parents forsook him, what does that mean? There was a history to that prayer. It first became evident that there was a strain in his family when David's father, Jesse, was called up by the prophet Samuel to gather *all* of Jesse's sons. God had instructed Samuel to anoint one of Jesse's sons as the new king of Israel. However, Samuel went through seven of Jesse's sons, and God said that none of them were the chosen king. So, confused, Samuel asked, "Are these all the sons you have?" (1 Samuel 16:11, NIV) Jesse said that he had one more. He was the youngest, and he was out in the fields working with the sheep and goats.

Picture this: Samuel had told him to gather *all* of his sons. Jesse gathered seven of his sons and did not invite David to stand before the prophet. How do you think David felt? How would you feel if your father did not believe you were worthy enough? Not only that, but Jesse did not know which of his sons was supposed to be king, so he was standing in the way of David's destiny. Thankfully, God the Father saw the worth in David that his earthly father could not see, and God the Father refused to allow the sins of a man to keep David from his calling.

Now fast-forward a few years, and David was serving King Saul. David admired Saul and looked at him like a mentor. David was deeply loyal to King Saul. He played his harp to soothe Saul, defeated Goliath, commanded armies, and won many battles for his king. He also had a deep friendship with Saul's son Jonathan. Yet, despite all the affection David had for Saul, that affection was not returned. King Saul was intensely jealous of David and resented him. Then the worst thing that could happen to David did. His mentor turned on him and tried to kill him. When David fled, he became the most wanted man in Israel as King Saul, along with his armies, pursued one goal, to end David's life. Imagine the torment in David's heart as he grew up being rejected by his earthly father and now rejected by the man he admired.

Whom can David trust? I am sure while David was hiding in those caves, there were moments when David asked himself that very question. However, as I read the writings of David, I discovered the powerful ways David learned to navigate the moments when imperfect people hurt him. The first thing we learn from David is that it is okay to share your feelings with God. For some reason, we think we have to go to God in our prayers with these stoic, put-together, poetic prayers. We feel like if we express our true selves to God, He's going to strike us with a lightning bolt or something. So we talk to God in these vague ways, like for some reason the Creator of the universe doesn't understand how we feel. David was raw and honest before God. When I read the desperation he wrote in Psalm 142, I can picture David face down on the cold, damp floor of that cave crying to God in prayer. He wrote:

> *I cry out to the LORD;*
> *I plead for the LORD's mercy.*
>
> *I pour out my complaints before him*
> *and tell him all my troubles.*
>
> *When I am overwhelmed,*
> *you alone know the way I should turn.*
>
> *Wherever I go,*
> *my enemies have set traps for me.*
>
> *I look for someone to come and help me,*
> *but no one gives me a passing thought!*
>
> *No one will help me;*
> *no one cares a bit what happens to me.*
>
> *Then I pray to you, O LORD.*
> *I say, "You are my place of refuge.*
>
> *You are all I really want in life.*
>
> —Psalm 142:1-5

Have you ever felt like that? Have you ever felt like no one comes to help you? No one cares a bit about what you are going through or how you feel? Have you ever felt overwhelmed by all your troubles and all your circumstances? What did David do? He poured his complaints to God. He didn't pour complaints to Facebook; he poured his complaints out to God. He didn't vent to the world; he vented to the Creator of the world. Why? Because David knew that God was his only place of refuge, and God was all David really wanted in this life!

We learn, secondly, from David that proactive praise transforms us. As you start reading the psalm David wrote hiding in those caves while in isolation, you begin to see David's perspective. He understood that for his problems to get smaller, his God had to get bigger. David had a shift in his spirit where, despite his feelings, he started praising and declaring who God is.

> *I cry out to God Most High,*
> *to God who will fulfill his purpose for me.*
>
> *He will send help from heaven to rescue me,*
> *disgracing those who hound me. . . .*
>
> *Be exalted, O God, above the highest heavens!*
> *May your glory shine over all the earth. . . .*
>
> *My heart is confident in you, O God;*
> *my heart is confident.*
> *No wonder I can sing your praises. . . .*
>
> *I will thank you, Lord, among all the people.*
> *I will sing your praises among the nations.*
>
> *For your unfailing love is as high as the heavens.*
> *Your faithfulness reaches to the clouds.*
>
> —Psalms 57:2-3, 5, 7, 9-10

It is so powerful to see how, despite the circumstances that David was in, he found himself in proactive praise. I call it proactive because we have conscious decisions to make in the midst of dire situations. We either wallow or we praise our way through our pain. In his book *A Long Obedience in the Same Direction*, Eugene Peterson drives this point home:

> I have never said that we worship because we feel like it. Feelings are great liars. If Christians worship only when they felt like it, there would be precious little worship. Feelings are important in many areas but completely unreliable in matters of faith. Paul Scherer is laconic: "The Bible wastes very little time on the way we feel."
>
> We live in what one writer has called the "age of sensation." We think that if we don't feel something there could be no authenticity in doing it. But the wisdom of God says something different: that we can act ourselves into a new way of feeling much quicker than we can feel ourselves into a new way of acting. Worship is an act that develops feelings for God, not a feeling for God that is expressed in an act of worship. When we obey the command to praise God in worship, our deep, essential need to be in relationship with God is nurtured.[3]

The last thing we can learn from David is that when God moves in our lives, we must share it with others. If you look at the story written in 1 Samuel during the time of David fleeing for his life and hiding in the Cave of Adullam, you'll notice that word in the region starts getting out that David is in the area. The Bible states that he started attracting these completely distraught men. They were in trouble, running from their debts, and were considered the outcasts of the area. They went to David to lead them and help them.

---

3   Eugene H. Peterson, *A Long Obedience in the Same Direction: Discipleship in an Instant Society*, (Downers Grove, IL: Intervarsity Press, 2021).

You would think that the last thing that David would want to do when he was betrayed and emotionally distressed would be to help other people. However, David became their leader and mentor while encouraging these men. He spoke into their lives and proclaimed that they could become valiant champions and warriors and they could rise above their pasts. How could David lead like this when he had experienced so much heartache dealt by the hands of the people he loved so dearly? David navigated his pain by sharing with God how he was feeling, and those honest prayers turned to proactive praise. As David was praising God, his problems got smaller, and his God got bigger. So when God started moving in his life, David did not hoard the move of God, but instead he poured it into the lives of those he influenced. Look at the words David wrote in Psalm 34:

> *In my desperation I prayed, and the LORD listened;*
>> *he saved me from all my troubles. . . .*
>
> *Taste and see that the LORD is good.*
>> *Oh, the joys of those who take refuge in him!*
>
> *Fear the LORD, you his godly people,*
>> *for those who fear him will have all they need.*
>
> *Even strong young lions sometimes go hungry,*
>> *but those who trust in the LORD will lack no good thing.*
>
> *Come, my children, and listen to me,*
>> *and I will teach you to fear the LORD.*
>> —Psalms 34:6, 8-11

Unfortunately, sometimes we are on the wrong side of people's imperfections. Even Jesus explained to His disciples that we would experience offenses, backlash, and tribulations. The old saying is true: hurt people hurt people. However, the same adage also applies: healed people heal people. We can navigate through the pain of being abandoned and betrayed and realize, like David, that God will always receive us with open arms most lovingly!

Sometimes we are on the wrong side of people's imperfections.

CHAPTER 8

WHAT LIE DO YOU HAVE TO BELIEVE?

These last several years have been a roller coaster of emotions. As an adult, I am experiencing relationships that I never knew could exist before. I have built a relationship with a therapist that has helped guide me through my difficult childhood experiences. I have also had a spiritual father, Pastor Scott Wilson, step into my life in ways that I have never known before.

However, to say that since Scott has entered my life, all the voids I accumulated over the years have been filled would be a bit of an exaggeration, to say the least. If I can be completely raw regarding him, I struggle with waiting for the other shoe to drop with Pastor Scott. I hold my breath, wondering when he will let me down like everyone else has.

If you ever have the pleasure of meeting Pastor Scott, you will meet one of the most affirming and loving people in the entire world. You may think that I am exaggerating, but I am probably *still* underselling how much he cares for people. Yet, it is so easy for me to look at him through the wounds of my past. I hear him speak such kind words over my life, and immediately my mind tells me that he does not mean them, that he's only saying them to be nice. Or I tell myself he says those things to everyone and that I am not special. With him, I live in a constant state of insecurity, and it is not because he has done anything to deserve that. It's simply because I do not know how to accept those things from anyone. I have spent my entire life seeing those I look up to let me down, and I just expect that he will as well—such a sad way to live.

Not only does Pastor Scott speak affirmations over my life and spend meaningful time with me, but he has also exposed me to opportunities that I had previously never been afforded. One of these opportunities was a golf event hosted by John Maxwell. I have read John's books since I was eighteen years old, and his teachings have mentored me for decades. To say I was excited to be at this event is an understatement. However, if you know me, you know that golf is far from being my forte. I expressed the disappointing nature of my golf skills, and Scott replied, "Don't worry about it. We are just playing with friends, and none of us are good." Now, there is a HUGE distance between my buddy's "not good" golf game and my "atrocious" golf game, but I decided to go anyway because it is still fun to golf with friends!

So the event launched with a beautiful dinner outside under a white tent overlooking the ocean at the Ocean Course at Kiawah Island in South Carolina. The food was excellent, the music was terrific, and we were having a blast. At the end of the dinner, they told everyone to check their phones as they had just uploaded everyone's tee times. I looked through the timeslots and found my name along with whom I was playing. I was in a foursome with John C. Maxwell! This couldn't be right. They had to have gotten two Michaels mixed up. I went over to Scott to rectify their innocent mistake and discovered that it was actually correct; John had asked to play with me along with two other gentlemen. I was freaking out—and not in a good way. It is one thing to be bad at golf with some buddies. It is another to play horribly with the event host who happens to be someone you have looked up to for decades!

All jokes aside, it was a wonderful day. Of course, I lived up to my reputation with my golf game, but I had a great time playing golf and eating lunch with that group. It was a tremendous honor. Unfortunately, I did not see it that way after the fact. You would have thought I would have been on cloud nine leaving that event, but the truth was that I let my insecurities rob me from valuing that experience.

I left that event and went home with a fake smile and a corrupted heart. On the outside, I acted like it was the best experience ever. However, on the inside, I was beating myself up. I was telling myself that John had wasted his time hanging out with someone like me. I am nobody, and he should have replaced me with a more high-caliber leader. On top of that, I started letting my insecurities pollute my relationship with Scott by not believing he meant those affirmations he spoke over me as I mentioned earlier.

In one of my therapy appointments, I shared what I was struggling with, and my therapist made a statement that has had a tremendous impact on my life. He said, "*What lie do you have to believe to make those negative feelings true?*" For my negative feelings to be true, the lie I had to believe was that John Maxwell was a gullible idiot, and the only reason he spent time with me was because I was able to get one over on him. The lie that I had to believe regarding Scott was that he was a fraud, compulsive liar, and manipulator to discount every good thing he had spoken over my life.

"What lie do you have to believe to make those negative feelings true?"

For something to be true, it always has to be true, and that's the game the devil tries to play in our lives. Jesus said it best when describing the devil:

> *He was a murderer from the beginning. He has always hated the truth, because there is no truth in him. When he lies, it is consistent with his character; for he is a liar and the father of lies."*
> —John 8:44

If we're honest with ourselves, part of the unhealthy thoughts that replay in our lives are the lies and manipulation we have believed. We have forgotten the good that has taken place in our past, we are not anticipating a healthy future, and we are settling for the lies the enemy has been speaking into our hearts and minds.

Read how Paul told us to react to the ungodly thoughts that swim in our minds:

> *We can demolish every deceptive fantasy that opposes God and break through every arrogant attitude that is raised up in defiance of the true knowledge of God. We capture, like prisoners of war, every thought and insist that it bow in obedience to the Anointed One.*
>
> —2 Corinthians 10:5 (TPT)

Do you feel Paul's intensity? Do you understand that to capture something and insist it bow in obedience will take force? Can you see the intentionality that will be required, but also the hope that every unhealthy thought can submit to the knowledge and nature of who Jesus is? In his book, *A Long Obedience in the Same Direction*, Eugene Peterson shows us several ways how we can attune our minds to God's truth and discover a heavenly joy!

DO WE TRULY FEAR GOD BY BEING IN AWE OF HIM?

> *"How joyful are those who fear the Lord—all who follow his ways! You will enjoy the fruit of your labor. How joyful and prosperous you will be!"*
>
> —Psalms 128:1-2

Do we have a reverence for God, a deep sense of awe in God? I love Eugene's boldness as he expresses that the Bible doesn't really care whether or not you believe in God; he claims that most people more or less believe that there is a God. The Bible and the authors of the letters of our faith express that what God cares about is our response to Him. Do we see Him as all-knowing, glorious, and wonderful? Do we see Him as vast and holy? Do we see Him as an unfailing God who loves us beyond our comprehension? Do we see him as the actual Creator of our lives, the Sculptor of our souls, and the Director of where we're going? Or are we trying to make him fit our small minds? Are we packaging God to fit the conveniences of our lives? Are we telling Him about the lives we want to be created for instead of surrendering to His created purposes for our lives. Are we just trying to find a faith that is conducive to our lifestyle, and only then, will we agree to serve God? We refuse to go any deeper. Or are we getting to the place where we say to God, "Not my will, but your will be done?"

Joy is only found in surrender because joy is rooted in your identity in God and the plans that He has for you. Is God enough for you?

Joy is only found in surrender because joy is rooted in your identity in God and the plans that He has for you. Is God enough for you?

WHAT IS REALLY IMPORTANT?

What are the wins that will matter a decade from now, two decades from now, or a hundred years from now? When you ask yourself the question of what is really important in life, it will cause you to reflect backward with celebration and look forward with anticipation in working towards something that truly matters.

> If God doesn't build the house,
>   the builders only build shacks.

> If God doesn't guard the city,
>   the night watchman might as well nap.

It's useless to rise early and go to bed late,
  and work your worried fingers to the bone.

Don't you know he enjoys
  giving rest to those he loves?

Don't you see that children are GOD's best gift?
  the fruit of the womb his generous legacy?

Like a warrior's fistful of arrows
  are the children of a vigorous youth.

Oh, how blessed are you parents,
  with your quivers full of children!

Your enemies don't stand a chance against you;
  you'll sweep them right off your doorstep.
                                    —Psalm 127 (MSG)

You have to grasp what God is saying here in this Psalm. The psalmist penned these words to get us to grasp the reality that we can work and try to build things all day long, but they will never be enough for us. We can do business with our own two hands, we can build wealth with our own two hands, we can achieve success with our own two hands, but it will never be enough. There's no earthly amount that will be enough for you. There's no growth in your business, number in your bank account, amount of recognition, or particular possession that will finally be enough for you. And the sad truth is that it will exhaust you trying to prove God wrong by striving wholeheartedly for those things.

Look at what the psalmist said here. He stated that *true blessings are found in pouring into the legacy of those that are coming after you.* If you are a parent, that means the most significant win for your life is what your children will be like ten years from now. In your workplace, the most incredible legacy you can leave is that the generation coming after you will be equipped to be better than you. That means we are spiritual mothers and spiritual fathers in the church, and we are discipling those that are young in their faith. The only thing that we can measure that is vital is that we are investing our lives into people, so they can be all they are created to be. The character of our work is shaped not by accomplishments or possessions but by the depth of the relationships we have. Eugene Peterson said it best, "We invest our energy in people. Among those around us we develop sons and daughters, sisters and brothers even as our Lord did with us!"

The character of our work is shaped not by accomplishments or possessions but by the depth of the relationships we have.

ARE YOU CARRYING THE WEIGHT ALONE?

As I have counseled, pastored, and discipled people for decades now, I have come across a theme in the lives of struggling people. This theme plays itself out in a series of thoughts that circle their minds as they tell themselves, *No one gets me. There is nothing someone can say or do to make this better. They do not understand how I truly feel. This is my weight to bear, and I bear it alone.* However, you are not alone, and you do most certainly have someone who understands you!

> *He was despised and rejected—a man of sorrows, acquainted with deepest grief. We turned our backs on him and looked the other way. He was despised, and we did not care. Yet it was our weaknesses he carried; it was our sorrows that weighed him down. And we thought his troubles were a punishment from God, a punishment for his own sins! But he was pierced for our rebellion, crushed*

for our sins. He was beaten so we could be whole. He was whipped
so we could be healed.

—Isaiah 53:3-5

The writer of Hebrews took these truths one step further as he painted this beautiful picture of how Jesus understands our weaknesses and temptations because He was tempted, just like we are, even though He did not sin. How powerful to realize that Jesus was a man of sorrows acquainted with the deepest grief because He freely chose to take all our weaknesses and sorrows upon Himself so that we could be whole and healed! However, though this gift of healing is free for you to take, it will never be forced upon you. You have to choose to give your burden over to Jesus.

Then Jesus said, "Come to me, all of you who are weary and carry
heavy burdens, and I will give you rest. Take my yoke upon you.
Let me teach you, because I am humble and gentle at heart, and
you will find rest for your souls. For my yoke is easy to bear, and
the burden I give you is light."

—Matthew 11:28-30

CHAPTER 9

THIS IS WHAT IT FEELS LIKE.

What do good dads look like? How do they behave? How do they interact with their kids and their spouses? These were the questions that filtered through my head as I was entering my late thirties. How do you know if you have never had a clear picture of that as an example? Where do you even find the answers to these deep longings of a man when you have not seen it modeled? You may know what you think you should be hypothetically, but tangibly, can you pull it off or honestly know what a healthy father is? Sure, you can look through the lens of pop culture and see the picture of a father that it portrays, but is that realistic or an over-exaggerated caricature? Also, if you have the wrong image or definition of what a good father is, how do you know if you are rising to the challenge or failing miserably?

I get it. I sound completely unstable and sporadic. Still, in the name of transparency, these were the questions that caused a lot of doubt regarding my capabilities as a father and a husband. I spent many sessions with my therapist wrestling for the answers and painting unhealthy conclusions that I was falling short in so many ways. However, one day my therapist asked me a question that completely changed my perspective. He asked, "How the heck are you doing so well?" He was basically assessing that on paper I was correct; my life should not be as healthy as it is. Based on my family of origin, my marriage, my relationship with my children, and my workplace success should be in utter disarray. Now, of course, my life is far from perfect, and the very reason I spend many hours in therapy is to be a better husband, father, friend, and leader. However, hearing him say that to me did resonate deeply in my soul.

You do not just magically wake up healed and whole; it is a process.

I will be honest that hearing that question was an important moment in my life, but the journey towards health is, in fact, a journey. You do not just magically wake up healed and whole; it is a process. I still struggle with self-depreciation and being my own worst enemy. I have told my therapist a few times that I feel like a "wuss," and I feel full of pity because I keep struggling with specific emotions. I get angry with myself that there are areas of my life that I have identified that are unhealthy, yet I still revert to them. I have told myself the gravest of lies that maybe I cannot be better. However, this is precisely why we need relationships where we can be vulnerable and authentic with our deepest emotions; then, those people can be voices of truth in our lives. No, I am not where I want to be, but I am a whole lot better than I could have been! According to the Word, I am not alone in these struggles. Paul, in such a display of transparency, penned these words to the Roman church:

> *And I know that nothing good lives in me, that is, in my sinful nature. I want to do what is right, but I can't. I want to do what is good, but I don't. I don't want to do what is wrong, but I do it anyway. . . . Oh, what a miserable person I am! Who will free me from this life that is dominated by sin and death? Thank God! The answer is in Jesus Christ our Lord.*
> —Romans 7:18-19, 24-25

Through the years, I've noticed qualities and commitments of what a healthy father or parent possesses that I have applied as accountability in my life.

A HEALTHY FATHER PROTECTS HIS CHILDREN FROM DISCOURAGEMENT

Paul gives us this directive in Colossians, "Fathers, do not aggravate your children, or they will become discouraged" (Colossians 3:21). Paul's word for *discouraged* implies losing heart, lack of motivation, spiritless, disinterested, and no purpose in life. It is a profound warning that Paul is issuing for us not to be the kind of father who raises that kind of person. Instead, we should develop a style of fatherhood that produces the opposite of discouragement. So how do we do that?

First, we must teach our children that there is a difference between happiness and joy, and we strive for joy! Happiness is fickle and fleeting. This term comes from the root word *hap* which means *chance*. Human happiness is dependent on the chances and changes in life. With this definition of happiness, we place our contentment on the whims of this world. Only the world and what it gives you can cause you to be happy, and as quickly as it is given, it can be taken away. Not only that, but happiness can be lost in a moment based on a circumstance. Think about how your day can be going wonderfully, and then one phone call, traffic jam, spat with your wife, or incident with your kid can cause the tides to turn and ruin what once was a swell day. Happiness, that fickle little thing!

However, joy is different. Joy is a heart thing. It is rooted in the mindset you possess. Viktor Frankl, who was a Jewish prisoner during the Holocaust and is one of my biggest inspirations, said, "Everything can be taken from a man but one thing: the last of the human freedoms—to choose one's attitude in any given set of circumstances, to choose one's own way." [4] Viktor talked about how the Nazis could take away all his human freedoms as they imprisoned him physically, starved him, assigned him grueling labor, placed him in inhumane living situations, and murdered those around him, but they could not steal his liberty. They could not steal his ability to choose how he would think and mentally respond to his environments.

---

4   Viktor E. Frankl, *Man's Search for Meaning: The Classic Tribute to Hope: From the Holocaust* (London: Penguin, 2020).

Therefore, he developed a deep sense of purpose and an even greater sense of joy from that purpose, even in the most unimaginable, grotesque situations. He became an inspiration to the other prisoners and even to some of the Nazi soldiers. His words remind me of David's beautiful words in Psalms, "You have given me greater joy than those who have abundant harvests of grain and new wine. In peace I will lie down and sleep, for you alone, O Lord, will keep me safe" (Psalms 4:7-8).

Can we be the type of parents that show our children our devotion to God even in difficult times? Can we show that we are not slaves to emotions but servants to our God and that even in the midst of extreme difficulties, we know God will work all things together for those who love him? There are enough quitters in this world and enough who leave when the going gets tough, but we are the examples of what standing firm in our GOD looks like!

> God saw a need in this world and created our children to be a part of the solution to make this world better.

The second way we protect our children from discouragement is to build off of Viktor Frankl's sense of purpose: to lead those we parent, both physically and spiritually, towards their God-given calling. We need to teach young people that they are not accidents or afterthoughts. They are not less important, but they possess a God-given calling to make an eternal difference in the body of Christ. They have been given spiritual gifts to make a heavenly difference as a part of God's community! We need to build their confidence not in themselves, but in their God and the identity God has for them! Our job is to reveal to them that God saw a need in this world and created them to be a part of the solution to make this world better than they found it. We must parent with the responsibility of knowing that we must disciple those we influence. We must do so in order to see the prayer of the writer of Hebrews fulfilled when he penned these words:

> *May he equip you with all you need for doing his will. May he produce in you, through the power of Jesus Christ, every good thing that is pleasing to him. All glory to him forever and ever! Amen.*
> —Hebrews 13:21

A HEALTHY FATHER MUST NOT MISUSE HIS AUTHORITY

Let's look again at Paul's words in Colossians, but I want to add the prior verse this time:

> *Children, always obey your parents, for this pleases the Lord. Fathers, do not aggravate your children, or they will become discouraged.*
> —Colossians 3:20-21

Children, always obey! Paul gave fathers or father figures a tremendous amount of authority. He was telling the children that they needed to submit to an authority figure in their lives. However, Paul was not saying that this authority is unchecked. He followed up the instruction to the children by saying, "Fathers, you may have this authority over those you parent and lead, but you also have a responsibility not to aggravate or provoke your children to discouragement."

This is a similar message he gave the church in Ephesus when he said, "Fathers, do not provoke your children to anger by the way you treat them. Rather, bring them up with the discipline and instruction that comes from the Lord" (Ephesians 6:4)

Have you ever heard the statement, "Do what I say, not what I do?" Yeah, that does not work, especially with young people. They will do what you do despite what you say. The most significant misuse of our authority is that we do not model the things of God; we just mouth them! How do you think our children will respond when they look at us and see that we make everything a priority over God in our lives? Our careers, our hobbies, and our activities all take precedence over God. God is a priority when it is convenient for us, and if it is not, then everything else is more important. We attend church when we feel like it, we don't have time for a small group, we don't feel comfortable serving, and we read the Bible and pray when we have a chance. Hear me clearly; if God is an afterthought to you, then most likely, He will be of no thought to your children when they grow up! I heard it said once that we can either be a great example or a horrible warning—the choice is ours.

Not only do we model what healthy priorities are in our spiritual disciplines, but we must also model what Godly character is, most notably how we treat people. Do we respond to people with the nature of Jesus? So many people look at this world with hatred and disgust, and if we are honest, many of those critical voices call themselves followers of Jesus, which is mind-boggling to me. I do not understand why we expect a world that does not know Jesus to act like Jesus, and then we are appalled when they don't. Of course, they will not act like Jesus because they do not have a relationship with him. So how should we respond to a world that is far from God? Well, Jesus gives us a great example here:

> *When he saw the crowds, he had compassion on them because they were confused and helpless, like sheep without a shepherd. He said to his disciples, "The harvest is great, but the workers are few. So pray to the Lord who is in charge of the harvest; ask him to send more workers into his fields."*
>
> —Matthew 9:36-38

What would our world look like if we saw people with less hatred and more compassion? What would it look like if we allowed that compassion to drive us to truly want what is best for someone? What if that was the "win" that drove our lives, not proving how right we are and wrong they are. I know that debating people to death will not change them, but loving them to life will transform them.

We not only start to model how we see people differently, but we must also display that our words follow suit. Great fathers are great affirmers. They champion, celebrate, and spur on those they love. Solomon was extremely wise when he stated, "Gracious words are a honeycomb, sweet to the soul and healing to the bones" (Proverbs 16:24, NIV). Affirmations are sweet to our soul, which draws us closer to our loved ones that spoke them. They also heal the wounds that are afflicted by this sinful world. Even the words we say under the guise of sarcasm and jokes can be damaging over time and provoke much animosity in our children. This is why we should never forget to be slow to speak. When we understand how much weight our words possess, we can fill them with words of affirmation and call out their greatness!

Lastly, one of the most incredible ways to use your authority is when your children see that you have vulnerable and authentic relationships. When you model that you can share your weaknesses with those that keep you accountable, you give those you are discipling the freedom and confidence to do the same. Our expectations are the same as God's in which He does not expect us to be perfect, but He wants us to be progressing. When we stumble, struggle, and suffer, we don't find ourselves alone, but we, instead, have surrounded ourselves with those that speak truth and life into us. We are created in the context of community, and healing is only found in the context of authenticity within that community. James so poignantly put it, "Confess your sins to each other and pray for each other so that you may be healed. The earnest prayer of a righteous person has great power and produces wonderful results" (James 5:16).

When we stumble, struggle, and suffer, we don't find ourselves alone, but we, instead, have surrounded ourselves with those that speak truth and life into us.

CHAPTER 10

I COULD HAVE BEEN MICHAEL JACKSON?

It was a Saturday morning—January 29, 2022, to be exact. I woke up and got ready to speak at our morning prayer service to close out 21 Days of Prayer and Fasting. Before I did, I opened my phone; I know that's not a good habit first thing in the morning, but I checked my email anyway. There was an email with the subject line "Your DNA results are in." For Christmas, I had received the AncestryDNA test kit and had been waiting weeks to get the results. I have always been fascinated with history and inquisitive about my heritage as there have always been vague stories that I wanted to research further. As I opened my results, I saw the list of matched relatives. I saw my mother listed and many of her family members. I saw names that I did not recognize that showed DNA matches, which made me curious. Then I noticed my father was nowhere to be found.

I knew he was in the system since he had taken the DNA test himself, so I scoured the results. Not one trace of any of his side of the family was matched to me. The knot in my stomach hit me so hard that I thought I was about to puke. I mean, I have had sinking suspicions all my life. People had always told me that my dad didn't claim me until I was three, and many of his family members said I was not his. Dad always joked that I was not his, and my mom had boyfriends, but my dad's way of showing affirmation was through his cutting remarks, so I never fully believed it. Now I sat here at thirty-eight years old, and everything I had ever believed was not true. Who am I?

I felt broken, I felt hurt, and I felt lied to. I felt betrayed, unwanted, and numb.

I pulled myself together and tried to compose myself the best that I could to lead our church through this prayer service. I cried out to God. I felt broken, I felt hurt, and I felt lied to. I felt betrayed, unwanted, and numb. All I could do was throw myself at the feet of Jesus. However, there was no slowing down as I had to preach on Sunday and lead a volunteer rally night on Monday. I felt like I had no reprieve to process all that had happened.

Over the next few days, I just kept exhaling these sighs. It was like I couldn't hold my pain in, and my body was releasing it in these groans. I was going through waves of emotion where I was fine one minute but was brought to tears the next. I was grieving in a way that I had never grieved. On top of all my grief, there were a series of questions running through my mind. *Who is my biological father? I am matched with a series of relatives I have never heard of that literally were born forty-five minutes from where I was born.* But what do you do with that information, and where do you start? How would I talk to my mom, who had issues with speaking the truth because of her mental illness? How would I tell my father, who avoided confrontation like the plague, that he was not my biological father, and he was right all those years ago? How would I manage all this pain I was feeling? I had all these thoughts running through my mind: *No wonder he never fought for me my whole life. No wonder he was never proud of me. No wonder he can write me off so easily.* Yet, in the midst of all those thoughts, I knew that they couldn't be true because I have adopted my children. I would never write them off, I will always fight for them, and I am filled with pride that they are my babies! Yet, with all that truth, I knew I couldn't escape the pain. Who am I?

Less than a month later, on my dad's birthday, I was at the OneHope yearly Hope celebration event in Florida, and the guest speaker was Christine Caine. I had never heard Christine speak in person, so I was excited for her to preach. However, I didn't know it would be a divine word. As she started speaking a very relevant message for the conference and affirming all that Rob Hoskins, OneHope's president, had expressed the night before, she took a turn, and I felt like her message was speaking directly to me.

She told a story of how, when she was in her early thirties, her brother received a letter from the government of Australia that he was actually adopted. He was at his mother's house confronting her about the letter. So Christine rushed home to be with her brother, and as they were all emotional, she said she did what every Greek would do in this situation, and that was to make some food. As she prepared the food, her mother told her, "Now that we are telling the truth, do you want to know the truth about yourself?" Then she proceeded to tell Christine that she was also adopted and that, as their father passed away years ago, he made her mother promise to never tell the children they were adopted. In those days, all adoptions in Australia were closed, so they never thought the truth would come out.

As Christine was speaking this, I heard in the tone of her voice the reverberation of that familiar pain that I felt. The pain of your whole life being flipped upside down. Everything you believed was different. Christine said she searched for answers and found the government records from child services talking about when her biological mother gave her up for adoption. The form stated "Child," and in place of a name was a number. In the government's eyes, she said, she was reduced to a number on a piece of paper. Then, there was a brief description of her biological mother. It described the mother as having no emotional connection with the child and no desire to mother the child.

So, based on the information that the world had offered her, she was a nameless person who was completely unwanted. Christine explained how that information was enough to make any person live a defeated life, but she said she does have something that many people do not have: a relationship with Jesus. In her prayers of distress, God brought her to a beautiful scripture that screamed love into my soul as she read it: "The Lord called me before my birth; from within the womb he called me by name" (Isaiah 49:1).

Yes, the pain of not knowing is real. Yes, the shock is real. Yes, the hurt I have received from earthly parents is real. But you know what else is real? It is that the way I was conceived by my earthly parents does not mean that God did not intentionally create me. The world may look at my conception as an accident, but God looks at my creation and knows He sculpted me with a purpose. My God called me by name. Every day of my life is written in His book. I am His masterpiece that was crafted in His image. I am not a mistake. I am not discarded junk. I am not unwanted. My God desires me. My God sees greatness in me. My God has filled my life with purpose. My God is my father.

The world may look at my conception as an accident, but God looks at my creation and knows He sculpted me with a purpose.

As you are reading this, I hope you understand this is true for you also. I know that you may have experienced your share of pain and heartache. People may have wronged you in ways that are unthinkable, and you may have felt completely betrayed, but I can promise you that the imperfections of people are not the true reflection of a perfect God.

I still have a million unanswered questions regarding my biological family as I am writing this. I reached out to my mother, and, as I suspected, she gave me no information. She reiterated that she could not remember being with anyone other than my father. To be honest, I was very hurt by her response. She made no effort to give me any direction. Instead, she started directing the attention on herself as she was upset no one was asking how she was feeling about all of this. It is a very confusing place to be when you find out a large part of your life has been a lie and get no information from the one person who could help.

Despite her response, I still had this insatiable curiosity to know the truth. So my sister and I went into investigation mode. We reached out to DNA specialists to help us understand the possible relationship I could have with people I had been matched with based on our shared DNA. Through our research, we discovered that one person I had a strong match with would have been a first cousin of my biological father, and based on the time and place I was conceived, we were able to discover who we believed my biological father would be.

The sad truth is that he passed away in 2005, but I was able to uncover a few high school pictures of his online. I stared—speechless—at those pictures. I felt like I was looking at myself. My whole life I had felt like I never resembled my father or my siblings, and all this time, there was someone out there that I looked just like. Through his obituary, we discovered he had an older brother and one daughter who is a few years younger than I am. I have been in contact through Messenger with his daughter, and we have discovered through DNA tests that she is, in fact, my half-sibling.

My half-sibling and I are still in the very early stages of contact, and I have no idea what that relationship will look like in the future, but I do know a few things about my biological father. I know his last name was Jackson, so I could have been Michael Jackson which could have made my life a little more interesting growing up. Also, from what I can tell, he was a rancher in Texas. There are many more things that are still unknown, and I do not know if I will ever find the answers. I do not know if he knew I existed. I do not know if my mom told him that she was pregnant with me, and, like my dad, he refused to believe it was true or if he never knew. I do not know the sound of his voice, what his personality was like, or what his sense of humor was. Sadly, I do not know if I will ever discover those answers which makes my heart extremely sad.

However, with all these unanswered questions, I do know a few things for certain. My therapist made a statement to me during all of this that I cannot get out of my mind. He said, "*Mike, you are never more known than you are right now.*" For many years of my life, I have questioned who my father was, and I have more answers now than I ever had. My wife has also encouraged me with the understanding that I will be able to relate to our children in a special way. They, too, were adopted and not raised by their biological father, and, tragically, their biological father passed away without them ever having the opportunity of meeting him.

I also know that life does not happen *to* you but *for* you—that everything we experience in this fallen world has the ability to make us better and stronger if we cast our cares upon God. Paul said it so perfectly, "And we know that God causes everything to work together for the good of those who love God and are called according to his purpose for them" (Romans 8:28). It does not mean you will not face disappointments and challenges, but it does mean that, despite those circumstances, God will work them for good if we place them in His hands.

My pain is my testimony, and it is a testimony of healing and restoration and the shaping of a heavenly identity. It is a testimony that can inspire others towards God's healing and spur them on to run after who God created them to be. Most importantly, I know that no matter what I have experienced, my God has never left me or forsaken me, and as David proclaims in Psalm 139, I can never escape God's spirit. I rest in the fact that He is my comfort and peace, and my lineage comes from Him!

CHAPTER 11

WHERE DO WE START?

This big question is, where do I start? Not only where do I start, but how do I go the distance to reach the person I desire to be? You may think that it seems impossible to change or even come close to becoming that picture of the parent, spouse, leader, and disciple that you aspire to be. The hard truth is that you are a long way off. The good news is that we all are. No one is perfect and no one will ever be perfect, but we all can be a little bit better every single day. Here is a truth you must never forget: God does not expect you to be perfect, but He does desire you to be progressing. We can all take steps to progress daily towards health. Our goal should be to feel a little better, respond a little better, and achieve a little more every day.

I am not a runner, so much so that I actually loathe running. I am convinced that people who say they love to run are either liars to others or themselves because there can be absolutely nothing enjoyable about running. Ok, that was a little intense, and I am being slightly sarcastic. However, I know one of the greatest elations for runners is pushing their bodies past a point that seems unachievable. To do that means they develop an endurance that can withstand more and more every day. There comes a point where mentally, they have to push themselves beyond what their endurance was trained for.

One trick I found that many runners use, which I thought was fascinating, is creating mental finish lines. They will be running and find a landmark within view and tell themselves that they just have to make it to that point. A mental switch tells their bodies they have enough strength to get there. Once they pass that "finish line," they search for another and another until they genuinely finish. We have the same mental strength to achieve progress in any area that may seem daunting initially, but we must understand that we finish a race one step at a time.

Create mental finish lines to run to. This discipline of running one step at a time is precisely what Paul was talking about here:

> I don't mean to say that I have already achieved these things or that I have already reached perfection. But I press on to possess that perfection for which Christ Jesus first possessed me. No, dear brothers and sisters, I have not achieved it, but I focus on this one thing: Forgetting the past and looking forward to what lies ahead, I press on to reach the end of the race and receive the heavenly prize for which God, through Christ Jesus, is calling us."
> —Philippians 3:12-14 (emphasis added)

Press on! No, you are not where you want to end up, but guess what, you can get there if you keep pressing on. If you keep focusing on that one thing. If you keep taking that one step! So, the question is this: how? How do we press on and focus on that one thing? Let's look at how we can take this one step at a time and one day at a time to get closer to who we were created to be.

IF YOU GET YOUR MIND RIGHT, YOU WILL GET YOUR LIFE RIGHT!

Let's go back to Paul for some advice on this matter. Look at what he writes to the church in Corinth:

> Don't you know that the runners in a stadium all race, but only one receives the prize? Run in such a way to win the prize. Now everyone who competes exercises **self-control** in everything. They do it to receive a perishable crown, but we an imperishable crown. So I do not run like one who runs aimlessly or box like one beating the air. Instead, **I discipline my body and bring it under strict**

control, *so that after preaching to others, I myself will not be disqualified.*

—1 Corinthians 9:24-27 (CSB)

What seeds you plant, you harvest.

Do you want every thought you think and every word you speak to become a reality? Do you want all those self-deprecating, doubt-filled, bitter, jealous, angry, pitiful thoughts to become a certainty in your life? I hope your answer is absolutely not. However, the truth is that they are becoming your reality because that is what you are planting in your spirit. What seeds you plant, you harvest. You cannot get Godly promises when you are planting worldly curses! It is a spiritual law, and, as the Bible claims, "God is not a man, so he does not lie" (Numbers 23:19). God does not break His spiritual laws and nature. Paul said that he disciplined his body and exercised self-control. Napoleon Hill said, "Self-control is solely a matter of thought-control."[5]

How controlled are your thoughts? What are you dwelling on because that will be what you eventually speak. Jesus' very words were in Matthew 12:34 (author paraphrase), "From the overflow of the heart the mouth speaks," which is solely tied to what you are thinking and dwelling on. Peter wrote about our call to live a holy life: "So prepare your minds for action and exercise self-control" (1 Peter 1:13). You have to prepare your mind to become the person you know God created you to be. Prepare your mind toward pressing on and moving forward. Prepare your mind to get to where you know you want to go! Your life can be filled with the good things of God. Listen to the beautiful life the Holy Spirit offers us:

5   Napoleon Hill, *The Law of Success* (Shippensburg, PA: Sound Wisdom, 2021).

But the Holy Spirit produces this kind of fruit in our lives: love, joy, peace, patience, kindness, goodness, faithfulness, gentleness, and self-control. There is no law against these things!
—Galatians 5:22-23 (emphasis added)

Did you see that? NO LAW AGAINST THESE THINGS! Which means no law of this world can override the spiritual laws of God. Despite where someone is at, you can love them with a love that is not of this world, but that is a heavenly love that Jesus possesses. You can have joy and peace despite the circumstances this world brings your way! You can have patience with God and people. The list goes on and on. What I am trying to get you to understand is that the world has to submit to the spiritual laws of God because they are under the authority of God's spiritual laws. But, here is the kicker. God will not force you to submit to His spiritual laws; you have to choose them.

The sad reality is that most believers never live up to their potential because they believe and confess things that are opposed to their created design. You may be reading this right now and think, *That is easy for you to say. If you knew what I had to deal with, you would not be saying those things. You are not walking in my shoes. You do not know the uphill battle I have to face, the mountains in my life. You don't know how I was raised or how destitute my financial situation is. You don't understand how bleak my future looks and the lack of available opportunities for me.*

You are right. I do not know your situation, and I am not trying to minimize what you are going through, but I am trying to breathe hope into your situation. Please understand my heart as I write this. When those are your thoughts, all that is going through your mind is death, death, death, death, death, and death, and all that will come across your tongue will be death, death, death, death, death, and death. I want you to see Jesus talking about this very thing with some of His disciples. "Afterward, the disciples asked Jesus privately, 'Why couldn't we cast out that demon?'" (Matthew 17:19)

Some of you are asking similar questions:

→ "Why can't I defeat the devourer in my life?"
→ "Why can't I get over my circumstances?"
→ "Why can't I find freedom?"
→ "Why can't I experience abundance?"
→ "Why can't I find joy?"
→ "Why can't I discover my purpose?"

WHY, WHY, WHY? Check out Jesus' response:

> *"You don't have enough faith," Jesus told them. I tell you the truth, if you had faith even as small as a mustard seed, you could say to this mountain, 'Move from here to there,' and it would move. Nothing would be impossible."*
>
> —Matthew 17:20

Notice Jesus does not say that you must have the size of faith that He has. He also does not say that you need the size of faith of the heroes of our faith from the past (from Scripture). He says you need faith the size of a mustard seed. Why such a small amount? *Because small things that are nurtured grow!* So if you get your mind right, you will eventually see that your life gets right! Here is the great thing...growth compounds. So as you start nurturing your mindset toward the right kind of thinking over time, you will see tremendous progress in your life. Not only do you have to be in a constant state of praising God and remembering all that He has done in your life, but you also have to drive out the lies, the negativity, the death that is swirling in your mind.

Paul's instructions were to "take captive every thought to make it obedient to Christ" (2 Corinthians 10:5, NIV). Notice Paul said it is a conscious decision to take your negative thoughts captive. You have to develop grit and self-control for this to happen, and remember what Napoleon Hill said, "Self-control is solely a matter of thought-control." So when those bitter thoughts start rising up, you say, "NO! I am a person of forgiveness, mercy, grace, joy, and peace," and you do not give those negative thoughts breathing room to take over your mind. You may think this sounds too touchy-feely or that it sounds too simple, but I promise . . . growth compounds, and over time you will see your demeanor move away from those thoughts that have kept you captive for so many years. Not only do we need to take those contrary thoughts—that are the opposite of who we are created to be—captive, but we must replace those lies with the truth.

PHYSICALLY WRITE DOWN WHO YOU WANT TO BE AND HOW GOD SEES YOU!

"For we are God's masterpiece. He has created us anew in Christ Jesus, so we can do the good things he planned for us long ago" (Ephesians 2:10). Do not forget the way God sees you, how you have been redeemed by Jesus, and that you were created with a purpose. Take some time to start specifically writing a declaration over your life. What is the kind of person you want to be known as. What are the qualities and character of said person? What is the purpose in life that you desire to live, and most importantly, who does God say you are? Write it out, and declare it over your life.

There is something powerful about reminding yourself who you are intended to be and focusing on pursuing that person. Paul, in another racing analogy, said it like this:

> I don't mean to say that I have already achieved these things or that I have already reached perfection. But I press on to possess that perfection for which Christ Jesus first possessed me. No, dear brothers and sisters, I have not achieved it, but I focus on this one thing: Forgetting the past and looking forward to what lies ahead, I press on to reach the end of the race and receive the heavenly prize for which God, through Christ Jesus, is calling us.
>
> —Philippians 3:12-14

No, you are not perfect. Instead of fixating on the negative, recognize that you are no longer the person that you once were. You have grown and learned from your past. Focus on who Jesus says you are, and press on reaching for the person you are intended to be. However, how do you know who you are designed to be and what to focus on if you do not spell it out for yourself? Also, what makes you think you won't drift back to your old ways if you are not declaring what you are running after. Intentionality is the only way to change your reality!

Intentionality is the only way to change your reality!

EXAMINE YOURSELF

Remember, this is all about intentionality, and part of being intentional is keeping yourself accountable. "Examine yourselves to see if your faith is genuine. Test yourselves" (2 Corinthians 13:5). We will have better days than others, and the goal is to learn from each day. Some days you are not as affirming towards others as you know you should be. Some days, you missed the mark as a parent or spouse. Some days, your discipline lacked; some days, you were in a funk. The goal here is to learn from these stumbles.

Ask yourself why you felt the way you felt, and do not settle with your first answer that wants to justify your actions. Instead, dig deeper. What was the real reason you were triggered? Why were you angry with that person, why were you being distant, why were you slacking off? Get to the nitty-gritty of what is tripping you up, because if you do not learn to remove that hazard, you will stumble again and again and again.

Also, doing this will cause you to be more intentional about moving towards healthy, positive choices the next day. You will build off the good things that you just experienced. What caused that relationship to be enjoyable, why were you having such a great day, or what was the cause of your motivation? You should look at your shortcomings and adjust for a different response the next day. If you were distant from your children yesterday, then be proactive with them today. If you were frustrated with your spouse, then understand the deeper "why" to the frustration and communicate that, so you will not go down that path again. If your negative thoughts hijacked your mood, then be more intentional today to take those thoughts captive and replace them with the truth.

DAILY RINSE AND REPEAT

Do not forget that growth compounds. You may feel miles away from who you want to be, but take the pressure to be perfect off of yourself, and remember a race is completed one step at a time. Every day just gets a little bit better. James Clear, the author of *Atomic Habits*, summed it up like this, "Reading twenty pages per day is thirty books per year. Saving $10 per day is $3,650 per year. Running one mile per day is three hundred and sixty-five miles per year. Becoming 1% better per day is 37% better per year. Small habits are underestimated."[6] Do not underestimate where you can be a year from now, five years from now, and a decade from now if you make the decision to daily take steps towards the healthy, vibrant, purpose-filled child of God you are created to be!

---

6   Mark Clear, *Atomic Habits: Let's Change Your Atomic Habits!: A Full Simple Guide to Break Your Bad Routines and Learn New Good Ones* (Scotts Valley, CA: CreateSpace, 2021).

CPSIA information can be obtained
at www.ICGtesting.com
Printed in the USA
BVHW050507100622
639353BV00005B/12